Who Wants Seconds?

SOCIABLE SUPPERS
FOR VEGANS, OMNIVORES
& EVERYONE IN BETWEEN

Jennie Cook

PROSPECT
PARK
BOOKS

Published by Prospect Park Books
969 S. Raymond Avenue
Pasadena, California 91105
www.prospectparkbooks.com

Distributed by Consortium Books Sales & Distribution
www.cbsd.com

Library of Congress Cataloging in Publication Data is on file with the Library of Congress

The following is for reference only:

Cook, Jennie, 1959-
 Who Wants Seconds? sociable suppers for vegans, omnivores and everyone in between / by Jennie Cook — 1st ed.
   p. cm.
ISBN: 978-1-938849-13-8

1. Cooking, American. 2. Dinners and dining. 3. Vegan dining.   I. Title.

TX725.A1C5759 2013
 641.5'636--dc23

                        2013022389

First edition, first printing

Designed by Amy Inouye, Future Studio.
Photography by David Kiang, except where noted in the Acknowledgments.
Illustration on page 200 by Marion Eisenmann.
Photo and styling assistance by Sheila King.

Rubber stamps by StudioMo; Steven Vander Meer at Meer Image; and Robert Tepper at American Art Stamp and Gourmet Rubber Stamps.

Printed in China on sustainably produced, FSC-certified paper.

ADVANCE PRAISE FOR
WHO WANTS SECONDS?

"Jennie has a great talent for building relationships around delicious food—
this beautiful book shares the spirit of her cooking."
— JAMIE OLIVER, author of *Jamie's 15 Minute Meals*,
The Naked Chef, and many more books

"Jennie Cook is the most talented caterer in Los Angeles. I've been lucky
enough to have had many fine meals she has prepared. Her dishes inspire
everyone from vegans to carnivores to come back for seconds."
— ERIK KNUTZEN, author of *The Urban Homestead*
and blogger at RootSimple.com

"A beautiful book full of intriguing recipes by a woman who cooks with
consciousness and love. I can't wait to try them out!"
— STARHAWK, permaculture leader and author of *The Spiral Dance*,
The Empowerment Manual, and many other titles

"I met Jennie at a high school in South Central Los Angeles working with
RootDown LA to bring healthy, delicious food to teenagers, and I found
her approach toward cooking extremely entertaining and convivial. In
her new book, the full sense of her joy and colorfulness—similar to that
of the many vegetables she surrounds herself with—has been brought to
life in the amazing illustrated pages and simple, delicious recipes. Jennie
is a treasure in L.A., and now *Who Wants Seconds?* shares with the whole
country her wonderful food and her passion for building community around
the dinner table."
— ROY CHOI, author of *L.A. Son* and chef/owner of Kogi Taco
and L.A. restaurants Chego, A-Frame, and Sunny Spot

INTRODUCTION 10
DINNER PARTY ADVICE

CHAPTER ONE
BORN TO PARTY 15

*Lessons learned at my parents' cocktail parties, the beauty of baked beans
and cabbage, and the joys of eating outdoors.*

RECIPES:
★ Peach Bellini ★ Chef Ma's Old Fashioned ★ A Pitcher of Bloody Marys
★ Chilmark Cocktail ★ Watermelon Hearts ★ Homemade Lemonade
★ Ginger Concentrate ★ Divine Summer Elixir ★ Burgundy Beef Stew
★ Slow-roasted Baked Beans ★ Asparagus with Lemony Mayonnaise
★ Homemade Mayonnaise ★ Roasted Vegetable Ratatouille
★ Sausage, Peas & Potatoes ★ Chicken Sausage ★ My Favorite Waldorf Salad
★ Grammy's Sautéed Apples ★ Aunt Anna's Corn Fritters ★ Mango Salsa
★ Wednesday Night Macaroni & Cheese ★ Classic Béchamel ★ Cole Slaw
★ Pickled Cabbage ★ Asian Miso Slaw ★ Italian Cabbage Salad
★ Sticky Toffee Pudding

CHAPTER TWO
Love in a Bowl : Soup 44
Feeding the Family

*I learned to make soup in my twenties, when I was a newlywed in New York
and could only afford lentils and white beans.
The tricks I learned then for survival led to some of my heartiest,
most-requested dishes today.*

RECIPES:
★ Practical Advice for Making Soup ★ Roasted Garlic ★ White Beans & Greens Soup
★ Tomato Basil Soup with Coconut Milk ★ Cape Verde Vegetable Soup
★ Best Ever Lentil Soup ★ Miso Barley Mushroom Soup ★ Albondigas Soup
★ Zuppa Pasta Fagiole ★ Sunshine Ginger Soup

CHAPTER THREE

CATERING CLASSICS 66
THROWING A BIG PARTY

*When I moved to California in the spring of 1984, I was immediately enchanted,
and before long I was launching a catering business.
I'm sharing the recipes in this chapter reluctantly,
because now everyone will know how easy my job is.*

RECIPES:

★ Sassy Raspberry Salmon ★ Exotic Salad ★ Balsamic Vinaigrette
★ Curried Cauliflower Salad ★ Cumin-scented Turkey Meatloaf ★ Creamy Gravy
★ Silver Palate Party Chicken ★ Honey Roasted Carrots
★ Green Beans with Chile Pecans & Sesame Dressing ★ Toasting Walnuts
★ Farro al Fresco ★ The Amazing Corn Sensation ★ Cinnamon Fruit Crumble

CHAPTER FOUR

Mothers & Sisters 89
A WORD ABOUT APPETIZERS

*My women friends have had a huge impact on my life. I've been cooking for them
since the '80s, and they have given me nothing but encouragement and love.
So I always try to give them what they like: potatoes, meat, and dessert.*

RECIPES:

Moroccan Lamb Tagine ★ Perfect Roast Chicken ★ Miriam's Lacquered Chicken
★ Sweet Barbecued Brisket ★ Potatoes Anna for a Crowd
★ Indra's Jaffna Potatoes ★ Roasted Potato Salad
★ Melissa's Peanut Butter Blondies with Coconut Chocolate Ganache

CHAPTER FIVE

SLOWING DOWN IN SPAIN 106
COOKING ON VACATION

My family rented a house in Spain with two other families one summer, and that's when I was reminded to slow down, relax, linger over the table, and make croquetas.

RECIPES:
⭐ Traditional Spanish Gazpacho ⭐ Classic Potato Croquetas
⭐ Super Easy Aioli ⭐ Basque Red Pepper Chicken ⭐ Arroz con Pollo y Paella
⭐ Tortilla de Patatas ⭐ Rustic Fruit Tart

CHAPTER SIX

Sustainable Suppers 124
7 Tasty Flavor Profiles

My jealousy of Outstanding in the Field and other alternative supper clubs inspired me to launch my Vegan Supper Club during the last two years of my restaurant. Here are my best vegan recipes, many of which I developed during that time.

RECIPES:
⭐ Quinoa Fritters ⭐ Creamy Mushroom Gravy ⭐ Sweet Potato Fritters
⭐ Vegan Cilantro Crema ⭐ Boozy Blackberry Balsamic Reduction
⭐ Massaged Kale & Quinoa ⭐ Fennel Slaw ⭐ Endive, Avocado & Potato Salad
⭐ Vegan Caesar with Nu Cheeze & Handmade Croutons ⭐ Sweet Potato Lasagna
⭐ Cashew Cream Lasagna with Spinach & Mushrooms ⭐ Savory Cashew Cream Sauce
⭐ Baked Polenta Marinara with Pesto & Tofu Crumbles
⭐ Quick Polenta ⭐ Vegan Pesto ⭐ Homemade Ginger Ale
⭐ Roasted Salt & Pepper Vegetables ⭐ Onion Bhaji ⭐ Pumpkin Pie
⭐ Coconut Almond Whoopie Pies

Chapter Seven

SUNDAY SUPPERS 156
A Balanced Dinner Party Table

*Create a balanced menu, set the table, light the candles, pour the wine,
and connect with your current-day family.
Trust me: It will become the most important part of your week.*

RECIPES:
★ Masala Chai ★ Blackberry Vodka ★ Minted Lamb Meatballs
★ Chicken Cacciatore ★ Pasta alla Checca ★ Wonderful Kale Waldorf
★ Feijoada ★ Slow-roasted Kalua Pork ★ Spinach for a Crowd
★ Arugula, Winter Squash & Meyer Lemon ★ Pickled Cranberries
★ Cauliflower Chive Latkes ★ Allison's Cookies ★ Funny Cake

Useful Information 184

★ Menu Planning ★ Food Swaps ★ Pantry Staples
★ What to Have on Hand ★ Vegan Staples ★ Pie Crust 101
★ A Guide to the Staple Recipes ★ Cookware Wisdom
★ A Guide to the Advice ★ What's Vegan ★ What's Gluten-Free

MY PEOPLE 192

Where I thank the many people who made this book possible.

INDEX 194

INTRODUCTION
The Evolution of an Eater

This is the story of the evolution of an eater. A good eater: me. Along with all of that good eating, I've had some fun along the way. Three decades of catering in Los Angeles has provided great entertainment. I spent eleven of those years in the cute little urban hub known as Culver City, where I was the owner of a darling restaurant, Cook's Double Dutch. That experience was also entertaining, as well as life changing and crazy making.

In 2008, I closed the restaurant and moved the Shoppe (that's what I call my catering kitchen) from Culver City to Glassell Park. When I closed the restaurant and had some free time on my hands, I heard a clear message: Stop gathering riches and learn to be valuable.

So I hooked up with Nat at the Garden School Foundation and started a cooking program with elementary school kids in the garden on Wednesday afternoons. I kept scheming and created a cooking competition for high schoolers called the Mystery Lunch Box Challenge. I persuaded other chefs to join me, and we taught a three-week course at Jefferson High and Crenshaw High.

For the high schoolers, I met them where they were at, creating recipes around accessible produce in neighborhoods where sometimes the liquor store is your only source of fresh food. In three weeks, each team cooked more than ten plant-based recipes and were exposed to twenty-five more. They loved it! It was evident: Getting kids together around healthy, delicious food makes everybody happy. It's empowering to feed others, especially food prepared by hand with love, and it's fun.

And this is how we will save the world. It's not the only answer, just one of them. No matter what you eat, every time you buy food, you are casting your vote for the future. There's no right way, no wrong way—we simply need to make mindful choices and be kind to ourselves and each other about those choices. We need to keep talking and connecting over food—doesn't that sound like the easiest plan for change you've heard? It's time to party!

Over the course of my career, I've worked with many amazing hospitality professionals. For us lifers, we cannot stop serving. We like to share, we like to have fun, and most of all we want our guests to have fun. We love our food communities, and we thrive on teamwork. We are the medicine the earth needs, but it's not just us—YOU are the medicine the earth needs. As Rumi wrote, "There is a field, I will meet you there." We are all welcome to this party in the field. It's important

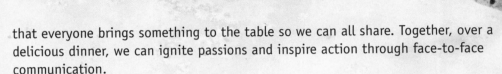

that everyone brings something to the table so we can all share. Together, over a delicious dinner, we can ignite passions and inspire action through face-to-face communication.

On my wedding day, my dad told me to err on the side of generosity. I was twenty years old, and it took me a while to understand what he meant. I've learned through the years that generosity fuels happiness, and now I know he was right.

This is what I believe. Writing this cookbook has been a project of the heart. From choosing the recipes to illustrating the pages, it's all been with just one goal: to ignite joy around your dinner table. Spread love.

Jennie Cook

GETTING STARTED

➤ Always read a recipe completely before starting—it helps with timing.

➤ I recommend grinding whole spices, but using preground ones if you're new to the kitchen is A-OK.

➤ Once you add salt to a bean dish, they won't get any softer, so cook them fully before salting.

➤ When it comes to the vegetables that make the deliciousness in a mirepoix, feel free to experiment with different combinations.

➤ I like olive oil and use it in everything. Grapeseed oil is a good alternative for a milder oil that takes a higher heat without burning.

➤ Above all, have fun. Turn on some music, sip a little tipple, and create something scrumptious. Anyone can cook.

Dinner Party Advice

"a party without CAKE is just a meeting"

Making a party great involves far more than planning a wonderful menu. The guest list should make you happy. The table should be expressive and inviting. And it's essential that you orchestrate the timing. A typical dinner party lasts three hours, more or less, and the meal should start no later than one hour after the first guest arrives. Set a beautiful table with all your serving utensils, trivets, plates, candles, and cutlery. If you need to procure a few forks or dessert plates, do it well in advance to lighten anxiety and fuel excitement. Make sure to have a bottle of bubbly chilling in case you feel the need to sparkle—I know I always do—and chill a pitcher of water for the table. When the first person arrives and asks, "What can I do?" show them the bar area and ask them to keep everyone's glasses brimming all night so you won't have to worry about that. Throwing your first dinner party can be daunting, so start small, no more than six, including yourself. Before you know it, you'll be entertaining like a pro.

Just don't forget the most important element for success—serve really delicious cake.

there CANNOT be GOOD living where there IS NOT Good DRINKING

Chapter
One
Born To
Party

HAPPY HOUR

Pops was a two-martini kind of guy. Straight up, with a twist, every night. I would patiently wait for him to finish and then fish out the gin-soaked lemon rind and savor every shocking bite. It wasn't uncommon for me to spill this mighty libation and then catch hell for being so clumsy; but then again, when that happened I'd also get an extra gin-soaked lemon rind. (Perhaps I was crafty, not clumsy.)

My family has always had a fondness for cocktail hour and day drinking. In moderation, of course, and why not? When Bellinis and Bloody Marys are the offering, and the occasion warrants a celebration, it's FUN.

And now, with all the hullabaloo surrounding artisanal cocktails and spirits, it's a great time to explore new distillations and to create your own signature cocktail.

Cocktail crafting should be easygoing and, above all, delicious. A good barkeeper is well prepared. Don't keep your guests waiting while you're squeezing fresh lime juice. Make big batches in sexy pitchers before your guests arrive, and don't take it too seriously—nobody likes a strung-out barkeep.

Make sure you have more ice than you think you need—we recommend three pounds per person at the catering company. I know, that's a lot of ice. Better safe than sorry, I always say.

At cocktail hour, my mom, also known as Chef Ma, is partial to Old Fashioneds, and I have a preference for sweet, pink, boozy drinks, as well as anything resembling Champagne, namely cava and Prosecco.

drinking champagne & making cocktails

peach bellini

The original Bellini was peach, but raspberry, mango, and strawberry are equally delicious. Just change the sorbet to match the fruit.

Peach sorbet, homemade if you're ambitious
Prosecco, cava, or Champagne
Fresh raspberries

Scoop a small spoonful of sorbet into the bottom of a Champagne glass. Fill with bubbly and garnish with fresh raspberries.

chef MA's old fashioned

Makes 1 cocktail

1 teaspoon sugar
Splash water
2 dashes bitters
1 pitted fresh cherry

1 orange wedge
2 ounces bourbon or rye whiskey
Ice

Mix sugar, water, and bitters in a highball glass. Drop in cherry and orange wedge. Muddle or smash into a paste using a muddler or the back end of a spoon. Pour in bourbon, stir, fill with ice, and serve.

martini ADVICE

➤ If you want a clear drink, stir.
➤ If you want a cloudy drink, shake.
➤ Many prefer a classic martini stirred.
➤ Cosmopolitans and fruity martinis are prettier with a shake.

a pitcher of bloody marys

I think tomato juice is an odd beverage, but Bloody Marys are not. Must be the vodka. This will make enough for lots of cocktails.

3 tablespoons Worcestershire sauce
2 tablespoons prepared horseradish, or freshly grated if you have it
2 tablespoons hot sauce (Tabasco or Tapatio or similar)
1/4 cup fresh lemon or lime juice
1 teaspoon celery seed
2 teaspoons freshly ground pepper
2 teaspoons sea salt
64 ounces tomato vegetable juice
Garnish: pickled vegetables, dill pickles, celery wands, or olives on skewers

Combine everything in a large, pretty pitcher and stir well. To make the cocktail, fill a glass with ice, add 2 ounces vodka, and fill the rest of the glass with bloody mix. Add garnish of your choice. This is equally delicious without vodka.

CHILMARK COCKTAIL

Makes 1 cocktail

Aperol is an Italian-made infusion of bitter orange, rhubarb, and an array of herbs, peels and spices. It's like a slightly sweeter, less alcoholic Campari, and the color is insanely fabulous. And since the alcohol content is relatively low, it's easy to drink. The classic Aperol cocktail, the Spritz, is made of Prosecco, seltzer, and Aperol, but try this version by my Martha's Vineyard chef friend Jeff instead. It's a rocking good cocktail on or off the island.

1 part Aperol
1 part St. Germain
3 parts sparkling wine
Basil sprigs for garnish

In an iced highball glass, pour in one ounce each Aperol and St. Germain. Top with sparkling wine to the top. Garnish with a sprig of basil.

how much BOOZE?

➤ In a 750 ML bottle of booze, expect to get twelve two-ounce shots, and assume one shot per cocktail.
➤ In a 1,750 ML bottle of booze (the jug-style bottles with the handles), expect to get 30 two-ounce shots.
➤ A bottle of wine contains four 6.5-ounce glasses.
➤ Allow two drinks per person at a typical party. If you're related to me, allow three. If all your friends are sober, allow one and make sure you have decaf coffee available.

A Shoutout to American Artisans

Our local vodka brand in L.A. is TRU, which marries organic American wheat and hand-processed ingredients to produce a quality drink. TRU is made by Greenbar, which also crafts bitters and liqueurs, all organic and sustainably produced, and it has some good cocktail recipes on its site. Another resource is Tito's in Austin, which makes fantastic small-batch vodkas. Check them out: www.greenbar.biz and titosvodka.com.

DRINKS DON'T NEED BOOZE
TO BE FESTIVE

WATERMELON HEARTS

One time, when I was a wee thing (but big enough to hold a butcher knife), I cut the entire heart out of a watermelon and ate it all at 4 o'clock in the afternoon. As a watermelon addict, I knew to go for the heart. Chef Ma was PISSED. I never confessed. (Until now—sorry, Ma!)

Watermelon is the only fruit that can go into a blender and come out as a thin and delectable juice. The color is a spectacular bright pink, and with some ginger concentrate and a little mint, it makes a divine summer elixir. Add it to lemonade, or freeze it into pops or ice cubes.

HOMEMADE LEMONADE

Cooking time: 15 minutes
Makes 1 gallon (16 cups)

2 cups sugar
2 cups fresh lemon juice
3 quarts water

Melt sugar and lemon juice together in a small pan over medium-high heat just until the sugar melts and the mixture is smooth, about 10 minutes. (Alternatively, combine them in a pitcher and stir until the sugar is melted, also about 10 minutes.) Remove from heat and mix in enough water to make 1 gallon.

The concentrate keeps indefinitely in the refrigerator. Mix with water before serving.

GINGER CONCENTRATE

Ginger is magic. I love all things ginger. My sister Rachel created this recipe for big batches of ginger brew to soothe a sore throat or to enhance an elixir. I like it so strong that it burns the back of my throat going down. It keeps indefinitely in the refrigerator.

Cooking time: 1 to 1 1/2 hours
Makes 1 quart (4 cups)

1 pound fresh ginger, unpeeled, sliced or chopped
4 quarts of water

Place ginger and water in a stockpot and bring to a boil over high heat. Reduce heat to medium and cook at a high simmer until reduced to 4 cups, about 1 hour. Remove from heat, strain ginger pieces from the liquid, and store in a clean container.

To make a cup of healing tisane, mix 1/4 cup Ginger Concentrate with 3/4 cup hot water and a squeeze of fresh lemon and sweeten to taste.

DIVINE SUMMER ELIXIR

Makes 1/2 gallon (8 cups)

3 quarts lemonade
2 cups watermelon juice
2 cups or more Ginger Concentrate
Ice
Sprigs of fresh mint, rosemary, or lavender

Mix everything together in a beautiful pitcher. Garnish with sprigs of fresh herbs.

 Burgundy beef stew

Here's the thing with stew: It doesn't need a lot of meat. It's all about the vegetables and the rich brown gravy. Chef Ma's stew was a simple classic. My hubs Johnny fell in love with my mom and her stew at the same time, and now she can't visit without making him a pot of this daube. My version has a little more wine than hers and a few more vegetables. Served over creamy polenta or barley, it's a comforting crowd pleaser and remains a family favorite.

Prep time: 30 minutes
Cooking time: About 2 1/2 hours
Serves 8 to 10

1/2 cup olive oil
2 pounds trimmed beef (chuck is fine),
    cut into 1-1/2-inch cubes
2 teaspoons sea salt, divided
1 teaspoon freshly ground pepper, divided
1/3 cup plus 2 tablespoons flour, divided
3 cups beef stock
5 garlic cloves, coarsely chopped
1 medium onion, chopped
2 stalks celery, chopped
1 pound button mushrooms, quartered, with stems
2 tablespoons tomato paste
1 tablespoon packed brown sugar
1 tablespoon Worcestershire sauce
4 sprigs fresh thyme or 1 teaspoon dried thyme
1 tablespoon smoked paprika
4 bay leaves

6 medium carrots, cut into 1-1/2-inch coins
1 750 ML bottle hearty red wine
Fresh parsley for garnish

Preheat oven to 325°. Place a large sauté pan over high heat and add 3 tablespoons olive oil. Season beef with 1 teaspoon salt and 1/2 teaspoon pepper and coat with 1/3 cup flour. Working in batches, brown the beef on all sides, transferring to a 6-quart or larger stockpot that will fit in the oven. Deglaze the sauté pan with 3 cups of beef stock, scraping up all the tasty bits from the bottom of the pan with a wooden spoon. Pour stock into stockpot.

Add 2 tablespoons olive oil to the same sauté pan and sauté garlic, onion, and celery until lightly browned and add to the stockpot with the beef. In the same pan, heat 1 tablespoon oil and sauté mushrooms until just soft and add to the stockpot. Stir tomato paste, brown sugar, Worcestershire, thyme, paprika, and bay leaves into the stew, then add carrots and wine. (Save the sauté pan for later.) Place stockpot over high heat, bring to a boil, cover, and transfer to oven, cooking for 2 hours. Test the meat; it should be fork-tender. If not, continue cooking, checking in at 15-minute intervals, until the meat is stew-tender.

When the meat is ready, thicken the jus with a quick roux. In the same sauté pan, heat 2 tablespoons olive oil or butter and stir in 2 tablespoons flour. When the roux starts to brown, add 1 cup liquid from the stew pot. Whisk to blend, then add 1 more cup liquid and whisk again. Allow it to thicken over medium-high heat. Pour over stew, stir, add 1 teaspoon salt and 1/2 teaspoon pepper; taste and add more if needed. Garnish with chopped parsley.

VARIATION: If you enjoy potatoes in your stew, add them during the last 45 minutes of cooking so they hold their form and don't melt away during the long cooking time.

BORN TO PARTY

Saturday Night Special

Every Saturday night we had the same meal: charcoal-grilled steaks, baked beans, home fries, and a salad. We always ate late on Saturday nights. Cocktail hour still started at 5, but the weekend pace was leisurely, pushing dinner till 7. This meant more time to dance in the kitchen. (As party people, we like to dance.) I loved watching Ma and Pop gently swing around the kitchen to Sinatra, with Ma harmonizing in her sexiest voice. I still also love a little piece of steak and a big plate of slow-roasted baked beans. Saturday night steak dinner will always have a hold on me.

Slow Roasted Baked Beans

You'll need to start this earlier in the day, but it can be left unattended in the oven for long stretches. Don't forget to soak the beans the night before.

Prep time: Overnight soaking
Cooking time: 4 1/2 to 5 hours
Serves 10 as a side dish

1 pound dried white beans, soaked overnight in 4 quarts water,
    drained and rinsed
1 tablespoon vinegar
3 sprigs thyme
2 bay leaves
1 onion, diced
1 cup dark brown sugar
2 cups tomato sauce (canned or jarred)
2 tablespoons Dijon or yellow mustard
Sea salt and freshly ground pepper to taste

Preheat the oven to 350°. In a large stockpot, cover beans with water by 2 or 3 inches, add vinegar, thyme, and bay leaves, and bring the beans to a boil over high heat. Reduce heat and simmer until beans are soft, about 1 hour.

Meanwhile, combine onion, sugar, tomato sauce, and mustard in medium bowl. When beans are soft, drain the cooking water, remove bay leaves and thyme stems, and stir beans into sauce mixture. Pour into a greased 4-quart glass, ceramic, or stainless pan and bake, covered, for 3 hours. Check and add more water, one cup at a time, as necessary, keeping it saucy but not watery. Uncover and continue cooking until beans are caramelized on top, 30 to 55 minutes. Taste and add salt and pepper if needed.

VARIATION:
Grammy added a pound of chopped raw bacon
to the pot, and I'd certainly understand
if you chose to do the same.

COLD ASPARAGUS with LEMONY MAYONNAISE

Asparagus is very clever. It grows straight up out of the ground and is a perennial. Year after year it reseeds all by itself. It's one of nature's tastiest miracles.

Our asparagus patch was at the top of the property. The bed was shallow, and the dirt was fluffy, so the spears could push through easily and grow to the preferred eight inches. Chef Ma would put on a sauté pan with a thin layer of water to boil. I would head up to the field with a colander and snap a pack of asparagus. By the time I got back with the goods, the water was boiling. The asparagus were blanched for a minute and then coated in, of course, butter. Try Lemony Mayonnaise instead. Mayonnaise is my favorite.

Prep time: 5 minutes
Cooking time: 3 minutes
Serves 4 to 6

1 bunch asparagus, about 1 pound, bottom ends trimmed
1/2 cup Homemade Mayonnaise (*see recipe next page*)
2 teaspoons fresh lemon juice
Zest of 1/2 lemon
2 to 3 tablespoons water
2 teaspoons sesame seeds (any kind) and diced green onions

Steam or blanch asparagus in boiling water. Skinny stalks cook as quickly as 60 seconds, and the chubby ones can take 3 minutes. Shock in cold water to stop cooking. Chill in the refrigerator, resting on a towel so it dries, while you make mayonnaise.

In a small bowl, whisk together mayonnaise, lemon juice, and zest. Whisk in 2 tablespoons water. Whisk in more water if needed until mayonnaise is pourable.

Serve alongside asparagus for dipping (or drizzle artfully on top). Sprinkle mayonnaise with sesame seeds and diced green onions or other herbs to garnish.

HOMEMADE MAYONNAISE

Prep time: 10 minutes
Makes about 1 cup

1 large egg yolk, room temperature (remove
   egg from fridge 20 minutes in advance)
1/4 teaspoon sea salt
2 teaspoons Dijon mustard
1 teaspoon sugar
2 tablespoons light-colored vinegar;
   lemon juice is also delicious
2/3 cup olive oil (or slightly less)

Put egg yolk, salt, mustard, sugar, and vinegar in a blender. (A hand blender or
old-fashioned whisk and stainless bowl will also work.) With blender on low, drizzle
in the oil in a tiny, tiny stream. Turn off the blender and check after 1/2 cup oil
is incorporated. It should be emulsifying and sticking to the sides of the blender;
if it's not, add a little more vinegar and blend or whisk again. Taste and add salt
if needed; if it's too tart, add more oil. If you like it, it's done! Remember, it's all
about the drizzle.

ROASTED VEGETABLE RATATOUILLE

Aunt Jean lived up the street, next to the woods. She was a vigilant gardener, on the ready to harvest her vegetables before the deer ate them up. This dish was one of her best. I should have appreciated it more at the time, but eggplant wasn't my thing as a youngster. Now I love eggplant so much I could marry it. This ratatouille stands alone as a delicious meal. Add a Caesar salad, a jammy Syrah, and a Rustic Fruit Tart (page 122) for dessert, and sit down at the supper table.

Prep time: About 30 minutes
Cooking time: 50 to 60 minutes
Serves 6 to 8 as a main course, 10 to 12 as a side dish

1 large or 2 medium eggplants, Italian preferred, peeled if you like
4 medium zucchini
1 cup olive oil
1 teaspoon dried thyme or 4 sprigs fresh, divided
2 red bell peppers, seeded and diced
1 yellow onion, diced
6 cloves garlic, minced
1 24-ounce jar delicious marinara sauce
1 cup hearty Burgundy wine (any varietal)
3 or 4 ripe tomatoes, cut into 1/3-inch slices
3 tablespoons fresh basil chiffonade*
Sea salt and freshly ground pepper to taste
1/2 cup Homemade Breadcrumbs (*see recipe page 37*)

*chiffonade = cut into slivers

Preheat oven to 375°. Slice eggplant and zucchini lengthwise about 1/3-inch thick. Arrange the slices in a single layer on 2 baking sheets that have been lightly oiled. Working quickly, rub or drizzle more olive oil on top of the vegetables. (Beware— eggplant is a sponge and soaks up the olive oil almost immediately.) Roast until vegetables are soft and a little brown on the edges, about 15 minutes.

Meanwhile, sauté peppers, onions, and garlic in 2 tablespoons olive oil over medium-low heat. When soft, add marinara sauce and red wine. Reduce heat to low and simmer on the back burner for 10 minutes or so while you prepare the casserole.

Coat a gratin or shallow 9" x 13" baking dish with 1 teaspoon olive oil and sprinkle half the thyme on the bottom. Place enough eggplant on the bottom to cover the dish. Arrange zucchini on top of the eggplant, then a layer of tomatoes. Scatter in some of the basil. Slather with 1 cup or so of the fortified marinara sauce. Repeat procedure, starting with the thyme, to add a second layer, like a lasagna, ending with marinara.

Sprinkle breadcrumbs evenly over the top and drizzle with a little olive oil. Place in center of the oven and bake, uncovered, until the juices are bubbling and the top is a deep golden brown, 30 to 40 minutes. Serve hot or at room temperature.

VARIATION: Omit the breadcrumbs and layer in sliced fresh mozzarella, ricotta, and grated parmesan (in whatever quantities you prefer) to make a gluten-free lasagna.

SAUSAGE PEAS AND POTATOES

This was the meal that made all the brothers and sisters happy. Chef Ma could feed all seven of us with a pound of meat and four potatoes; it was magic. Add a stack of white bread, some pickled cabbage, and a pitcher of whole milk, and there you have it: an American dinner, 1970s style. It's halfway between a hash and a stew, and when quality sausage is in the mix, its simple tastiness is heartwarming.

Prep time: 30 minutes
Cooking time: About 45 minutes
Serves 4 to 7

1 pound of your favorite raw sausage, loose or removed from casings and
   rolled into little meatballs (about 25 mini meatballs)
1 onion, diced
1 cup water, plus more as needed
1 tablespoon flour
4 medium red potatoes (about 1 1/2 pounds), unpeeled, diced into cubes
1 cup frozen peas
1/4 bunch fresh parsley, minced

In a large sauté pan with a lid, brown sausage over medium heat. Remove from pan and set aside. Leave just enough fat in the pan to sauté onion until translucent, about 7 minutes. Deglaze by adding 1/2 cup water to the pan and scraping up all the tasty bits with a wooden spoon. Whisk in flour to make a thin gravy, adding up to 1 cup more water as necessary to make the consistency that of a light gravy. Add potatoes, cover pan, and simmer over low heat for 20 minutes. Add sausage back to the pan. Continue cooking until potatoes and sausage are cooked through and the gravy thickens up. Stir in frozen peas and cook for 2 more minutes. Remove from heat and serve.

VARIATION:
This recipe is easily updated by substituting
stemmed and chopped kale for the peas.

30

MAKING SAUSAGE

A great way to know what you're eating is to make your own. Sausage is simple. Keep it fatty and make it spicy, then fry it up in a pan. You are now a sausage maker. Don't bother with casings—just patty it up. If you can't find granulated garlic and onion, try www.penzeys.com.

CHICKEN SAUSAGE

Prep time: 20 to 25 minutes
Makes 1 to 1 1/2 pounds

1 tablespoon paprika
1/2 teaspoon cayenne
1 teaspoon sea salt
1 teaspoon crushed red chile flakes
1/2 teaspoon dried oregano
1/2 teaspoon dried thyme
1/2 teaspoon freshly ground pepper
1 teaspoon granulated onion
1 teaspoon granulated garlic
1 pound boneless and skinless chicken thighs, chopped
5 cloves garlic, chopped

In a small bowl, combine paprika, cayenne, salt, chile flakes, oregano, thyme, pepper, and granulated onion and garlic and mix well to combine. Place chicken and chopped garlic in a larger bowl, sprinkle on the seasoning mixture, and mix with your hands or a spoon until the seasonings are evenly distributed. Cover and refrigerate at least 2 hours or up to 24 hours. The longer it sits, the stronger the flavors! Grind the seasoned meat in a meat grinder twice, or pulse in a food processor until it's minced. (I do it in a mini food processor in small batches.) Shape into little patties or meatballs and use it in any dish that calls for sausage or ground meat.

VARIATION: Feel free to substitute lamb or pork for the chicken.

the fruitery

We had a little grove of fruit trees in our upper field that never seemed to get the love it deserved. There was a cherry tree, two pears, and three apples, two of which bore fruit only on one side. The largest apple tree held a homemade fort with a life-threatening ladder. Predictably, I was forbidden entry until my older brothers moved on to go-carts and lost interest. The cherry tree was too high to climb, so most of the cherries went to the birds. The pear trees were short, old and pruned into mutant shapes. Chef Ma worked several seasons perfecting her pear-in-a-bottle growing techniques, which made the crippled trees look like they were suffering from boils.

Most of our apples fell to the ground before they were ripe. They were oddly shaped and more sour than sweet, but this didn't stop my Grammy (she lived with us) from putting them up every September. We'd collect the misshapen fruit in bushel baskets and she'd boil them up whole, all day long. She'd add a ton of sugar and strain it through a chinois-style food mill and bottle pints and pints of applesauce—delicious, sugary applesauce, best eaten on a piece of white bread and topped with lots of ground cinnamon. We had the best apple trees ever.

my favorite waldorf salad

A Waldorf is kind of like cole slaw for apples. It's an old fashioned recipe that really needs to make a comeback. I eat this for dinner on a bed of greens, topped with a drizzle of balsamic. Delish.

Prep time: 10 minutes
Makes 1 quart, or about 6 servings

6 apples, unpeeled, chopped in 1/2-inch pieces
2 celery stalks, sliced thin
1/2 cup toasted walnuts
1/2 cup dried cranberries
1 cup nonfat plain Greek yogurt
2 tablespoons sugar, honey, or agave

Mix everything together, chill, and enjoy.

grammy's sautéed apples

I love applesauce, but this is a much better use for apples. It's fresher, there's less sugar, and it's still a hit with the kids. One teaspoon ground cinnamon can be substituted for the sticks, but the sticks lend a deeper flavor.

Prep time: 5 minutes
Cooking time: 15 minutes
Serves 3 to 4

3 tablespoons butter or olive oil
2 cinnamon sticks, broken into 2 pieces about 3 inches long
6 firm apples, peeled if you like and sliced thin or thick (chef's choice)
2 tablespoons maple syrup
2 tablespoons sugar

Lightly heat butter or oil with cinnamon sticks in a large sauté pan, add apples, and stir to coat. Cook over medium-high heat, stirring, until apples start to brown and soften, about 8 minutes. Add maple syrup and sugar and continue cooking and stirring until caramelized, 7 to 8 minutes. Serve warm or at room temperature.

BERRY GOOD

One time, Aunt Jean and I went into the woods and picked wild berries and ate them on the spot. She called them wine berries; they were black and shiny and I loved them. When I told Chef Ma, she told me to never ever ever eat berries from the woods again. I didn't listen.

Aunt Anna's Corn Fritters

Corn on the cob was everybody's favorite vegetable in August. We rolled it in butter and covered it in salt. With the leftovers (Chef Ma always made a few extra cobs), she made corn fritters and slathered them with—of course—butter and maple syrup. The corn can be cooked or raw. I make silver-dollar-size fritters and serve them as an appetizer with Mango Salsa. People love 'em! If you like them with more batter, add less corn, and if you feel inspired, separate the yolks and beat the whites to stiff peaks and fold them in as the last step. This makes them fluffier.

Prep time: 10 to 15 minutes
Cooking time: 5 to 10 minutes
Makes about 12 3-inch fritters

1/4 cup flour
1 teaspoon sea salt
1/8 teaspoon pepper, any color
1 teaspoon baking powder
2 tablespoons milk, plus
   more as needed

2 eggs, lightly beaten
1 to 2 cups corn, freshly cut from the cob
2 tablespoons olive oil, plus more if needed
Maple syrup or Mango Salsa (*see next page*)

Sift together dry ingredients in a large bowl. In a smaller bowl, mix milk, eggs, and 1 cup corn. Lightly fold wet mixture into dry. Do not overmix or your fritters will be chewy (worse things could happen, just be aware). Add additional corn for a cornier fritter.

Heat large sauté pan over medium heat and add just enough oil to cover the bottom. Drop batter into pan with a large tablespoon and cook like a pancake over medium-high heat, about 2 minutes on each side. You can cook a few at a time, but allow room for spreading. Once the edges are sizzling, flip fritters and cook other side until cooked through and the middle is fluffy. Total cooking time is about 5 minutes per batch.

Meanwhile, in a little saucepan on the back burner, heat up some water and let the bottle of maple syrup sit in there and get warm.

If you're serving a crowd, you can scale the recipe up and make the fritters in batches, holding them in a 250-degree oven.

Mango Salsa

Prep time: 15 minutes
Makes 2 cups

1 large ripe mango, peeled, seeded, and chopped
1/4 cup seeded and finely chopped red bell pepper
2 tablespoons finely chopped red or green onion
1/2 bunch cilantro, chopped (leaves and stems)
1/2 fresh jalapeño, finely chopped, seeds removed for less heat
1 tablespoon honey
Juice of 1/2 orange
Juice of 1/2 lemon or lime
Sea salt to taste
Splash of hot sauce or more to taste

Combine all ingredients in a mixing bowl. Taste and add salt and
hot sauce as desired. Store in a covered container in the refrigerator.

**High school kids in a Root Down LA program made these corn fritters.
Aren't they beautiful?**

BORN TO PARTY

Wednesday Night Macaroni and Cheese

Chef Ma and Pops went out every Wednesday night. They'd get dressed up and have a date at the fancy French restaurant down the pike. We kids stayed home and ate mac 'n cheese with ketchup at the kitchen table. I still love a classic cheddar mac more than any other. But don't let my preferences stop you from trying something new. Add bacon, mix up the cheese varieties, drizzle it with truffle oil—these are all delicious options.

For this recipe, it's better to have a thinner sauce, because the cheese adds density as it bakes. A good mac 'n cheese has to start with a slightly al dente noodle and a well-seasoned white sauce. I love it with a toasted breadcrumb crust.

Prep time: 20 minutes
Cooking time: 30 to 45 minutes, plus time to cook pasta and Béchamel
Serves 8 as a main course, 12 to 15 as a side dish

1 pound pasta of choice (I like orecchiette or penne)
4 cups Classic Béchamel (see recipe next page)
6 cups (about 1 1/2 pounds) grated sharp white cheddar cheese
   (or other cheese if preferred)
1 teaspoon sea salt
1/2 teaspoon freshly ground pepper
1/2 cup Homemade Breadcrumbs (see recipe next page)
Olive oil to taste

Preheat oven to 350°. Boil pasta and cook until al dente. Leave it to drain in the sink while you make the Classic Béchamel.

When Béchamel is complete, grease 4-quart baking dish with butter or oil. In a large bowl, mix cooked pasta, 3 cups Béchamel, and 5 cups cheese and mix well. Taste a noodle and add salt and pepper to taste. Pour into greased baking dish. Top with 1 cup Béchamel and 1 cup cheese and push them into the casserole a little bit. Add breadcrumbs evenly on top and drizzle with olive oil to taste. Bake until sauce is bubbly and the dish is golden brown, 30 to 45 minutes.

WHO WANTS SECONDS?

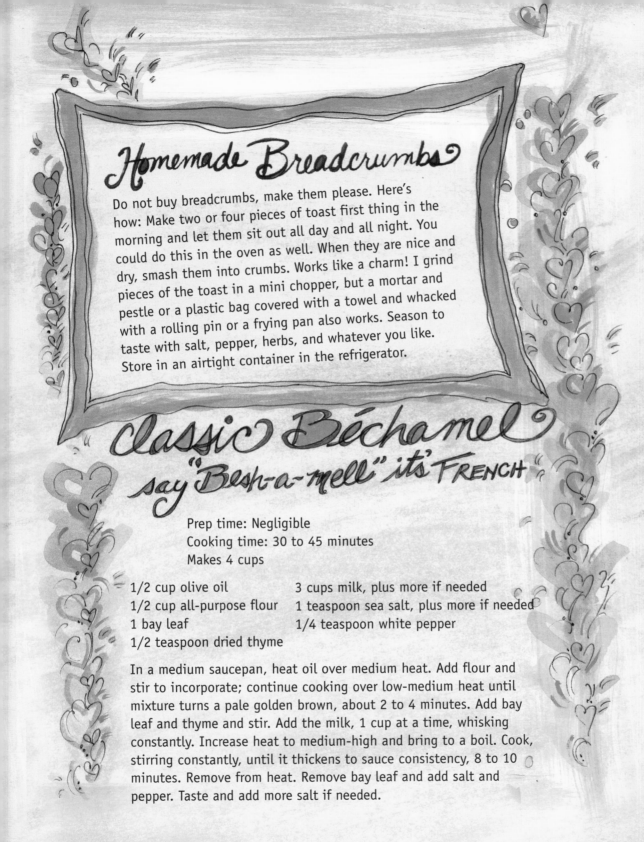

Homemade Breadcrumbs

Do not buy breadcrumbs, make them please. Here's how: Make two or four pieces of toast first thing in the morning and let them sit out all day and all night. You could do this in the oven as well. When they are nice and dry, smash them into crumbs. Works like a charm! I grind pieces of the toast in a mini chopper, but a mortar and pestle or a plastic bag covered with a towel and whacked with a rolling pin or a frying pan also works. Season to taste with salt, pepper, herbs, and whatever you like. Store in an airtight container in the refrigerator.

classic Béchamel
say "Besh-a-mell" it's FRENCH

Prep time: Negligible
Cooking time: 30 to 45 minutes
Makes 4 cups

1/2 cup olive oil
1/2 cup all-purpose flour
1 bay leaf
1/2 teaspoon dried thyme

3 cups milk, plus more if needed
1 teaspoon sea salt, plus more if needed
1/4 teaspoon white pepper

In a medium saucepan, heat oil over medium heat. Add flour and stir to incorporate; continue cooking over low-medium heat until mixture turns a pale golden brown, about 2 to 4 minutes. Add bay leaf and thyme and stir. Add the milk, 1 cup at a time, whisking constantly. Increase heat to medium-high and bring to a boil. Cook, stirring constantly, until it thickens to sauce consistency, 8 to 10 minutes. Remove from heat. Remove bay leaf and add salt and pepper. Taste and add more salt if needed.

WHY CABBAGE?

Chef Ma wasn't big on vegetables in the wintertime, but we always had a green salad, plenty of potatoes, and a little bowl of pickled cabbage on the dinner table. We never had a pork roast without sauerkraut, naturally sweetened with grated apple. My favorite cabbage was on Saint Patrick's Day, when every child got a huge wedge of boiled cabbage next to neon-pink corned beef and boiled potatoes. We doused it in vinegar and gobbled it up.

In the summer, we ate our family meals outside on the patio. The redwood picnic table was properly set, we still broke our bread before we buttered it, and we still had to ask to be excused, but it was liberating to be seated outdoors.

At the peak of summer, when the humidity was the most unbearable, Chef Ma would make us Cold Supper. Pa liked his suppers hot, and Chef Ma obliged him most times, so Cold Supper was a rare treat. It was simple, just a delicious combination of salads: tuna salad, chicken salad, fruit salad, potato salad, and slaw. Sometimes she'd add corn fritters so Pa had something hot. To me, this was the best dinner in the whole world.

As a grownup, I still love cabbage salads. They're versatile and sturdy. Although I hate the term "super food," cabbage is a top-five contender. I urge you to prepare it in a variety of ways and to try different kinds of cabbages. It keeps a good long time in the crisper and holds well after preparation. It's also crazy affordable all the time, not to mention hearty and plentiful. If you like a marinated (some might say soggy) salad like I do, let the cabbage slaw sit a day in the refrigerator to blend all those delicious flavors.

One large head of cabbage will make 12 to 15 servings of cabbage salad.

COLE SLAW

Plain yogurt or any combination of creamy condiment can be substituted for the mayo and sour cream. I've made it with all sorts of blends, and they've all been successful.

Prep time: 20 minutes
Makes 2 quarts (serves about 12)

1 pound thinly sliced cabbage,
  mixed colors preferred
2 large carrots, scrubbed and shredded
Leaves of 1/2 to 1 bunch parsley, minced
1/2 cup Homemade Mayonnaise
  (*see recipe page 27*)
1/2 cup sour cream

2 tablespoons Dijon mustard
2 tablespoons sugar
2 tablespoons cider vinegar
1 teaspoon celery seed
1 teaspoon granulated onion
1/2 teaspoon sea salt
1/2 teaspoon white pepper

Combine cabbage and carrots in a large bowl and set aside.

Combine all remaining ingredients in a medium bowl and whisk until smooth. Pour over vegetables. Allow to sit for about an hour at room temperature to blend flavors, then chill until ready to serve.

PICKLED CABBAGE

Prep time: 20 to 30 minutes
Makes about 2 quarts (serves about 12)

1 pound white or red cabbage
3 stalks celery, thinly sliced
2 bell peppers, seeded and chopped
1/2 red onion, grated
1/2 bunch parsley, minced
1/2 cup cider vinegar
1/2 cup hot water
1/4 cup sugar
1 tablespoon mustard seed
1 tablespoon celery seed

Combine cabbage, celery, peppers, onion, and parsley in a large bowl and set aside.

Combine remaining ingredients in a small saucepan. Place over medium heat and cook just enough to melt the sugar. Pour over vegetables, give it all a good stir, and allow to sit at room temperature for 30 minutes before refrigerating.

ASIAN MISO SLAW

Napa cabbage gets soggier quicker than a traditional cabbage; if you like your slaw crispy, hold the dressing on the side and toss the salad 15 minutes before serving.

Prep time: 20 to 30 minutes
Makes about 2 quarts (serves about 12)

1 pound napa cabbage (about 1/2 head), thinly sliced
4 carrots, shredded with a vegetable peeler or sliced thinly with a mandoline
3 green onions, julienned or sliced into circles
1 cup roasted peanuts
1 tablespoon sesame seeds, toasted or untoasted

1/4 cup miso
1 tablespoon Dijon mustard
3 tablespoons sugar
1/4 cup rice vinegar
1/4 cup tahini or peanut butter (or a mix of both!)
2 teaspoons sesame oil
2 tablespoons soy sauce
1 tablespoon grated ginger
4 cloves garlic, minced
1/2 jalapeño, minced, or chile flakes to taste

Combine cabbage, carrots, green onions, peanuts, and sesame seeds in large bowl and set aside. Combine all dressing ingredients in a medium bowl or a blender and whisk or blend until smooth. If it needs a little tang, add additional rice vinegar; if it needs to be creamier, add more nut butter or some coconut milk. Pour over vegetables, stir, and chill until you're ready to enjoy it.

VARIATION:
Add sliced apples and swap the peanuts
for walnuts.

ITALIAN CABBAGE SALAD

Prep time: 20 to 30 minutes
Makes about 3 quarts (serves about 18)

1/2 pounds red cabbage (about 3/4 head), thinly sliced
1 medium onion, thin! thin! thinly sliced
2 bell peppers, thin! thin! thinly sliced
2 carrots, shredded with a peeler, not a grater
2 tablespoons capers or chopped olives
1/2 bunch Italian parsley, leaves only, minced
1/2 cup extra-virgin olive oil
1/2 cup red wine vinegar
1 tablespoon minced garlic
1 teaspoon sea salt
1 tablespoon Dijon mustard
1/2 teaspoon chile flakes

Combine cabbage, onion, peppers, carrots, capers, and parsley in a large
bowl and set aside. Combine remaining ingredients in a medium bowl and
stir to mix. Pour over salad and stir to combine. Leave at room temperature
for at least an hour before refrigerating or eating, so the flavors can absorb.

Pickled Cabbage, page 39

STICKY TOFFEE PUDDING

Prep time: 40 minutes
Cooking time: 40 to 50 minutes, plus 10 minutes for Toffee Sauce
Serves 10 to 12

2 1/2 cups pitted and chopped dates
2 cups water
1 teaspoon baking soda
8 tablespoons butter, softened
3/4 cup sugar
1 tablespoon vanilla extract
3 eggs
1 3/4 cups flour
2 teaspoons baking powder
1 teaspoon sea salt
Toffee Sauce
2 cups whipped cream

Place dates and water in
a saucepan with a lid and
bring to a boil. Reduce
heat to medium and break
up dates, working into a
loose paste like applesauce, 10
to 15 minutes. Stir in the baking
soda, cover, remove from heat, and
allow to cool. Can be made a day ahead.

Preheat oven to 350°. Generously grease a 9-inch tube pan
or 9" x 13" baking dish. Meanwhile, cream butter, sugar, and vanilla together in
an electric mixer. Add eggs one at a time, mixing after each addition. Stir in flour,
baking powder, and salt. Add date mixture and stir to combine; it should be a
pouring consistency. Pour into prepared pan and bake until the cake springs back,
about 40 minutes (make sure to test—sometimes it needs an extra 10 minutes).
Invert cake on a plate and allow to cool while you prepare Toffee Sauce.

Poke holes in the cake with a skewer and pour half of the Toffee Sauce over the
cooled cake. Return to oven for 2 minutes so sauce melts into cake. Serve with more
Toffee Sauce on the side and a dollop of whipped cream.

 WHO WANTS SECONDS?

Christmas was a big holiday on the homestead. We made cookies for weeks. Chef Ma stored them stacked in Tupperware in the laundry room, tempting us kids daily. We always had a Christmas eve party, and all the moms brought more cookies—a Christmas miracle.

Today, we carry on the tradition in Echo Park, with the addition of wandering around the neighborhood caroling. It's the most memorable part of our year, and I honor it in part by baking this Sticky Toffee Pudding, making sure to have enough for breakfast leftovers on Christmas morning. I top it with heavy cream and extra Toffee Sauce. Extra sauce needs to be reheated before serving to melt the sugar crystals.

TOFFEE SAUCE

Prep time: Hardly any
Cooking time: 10 minutes

2 cups heavy cream or coconut milk
2 cups brown sugar

Combine cream and sugar in small saucepan, whisk, and bring to a boil. Reduce heat and cook, stirring every few minutes, until thickened, about 8 to 10 minutes.

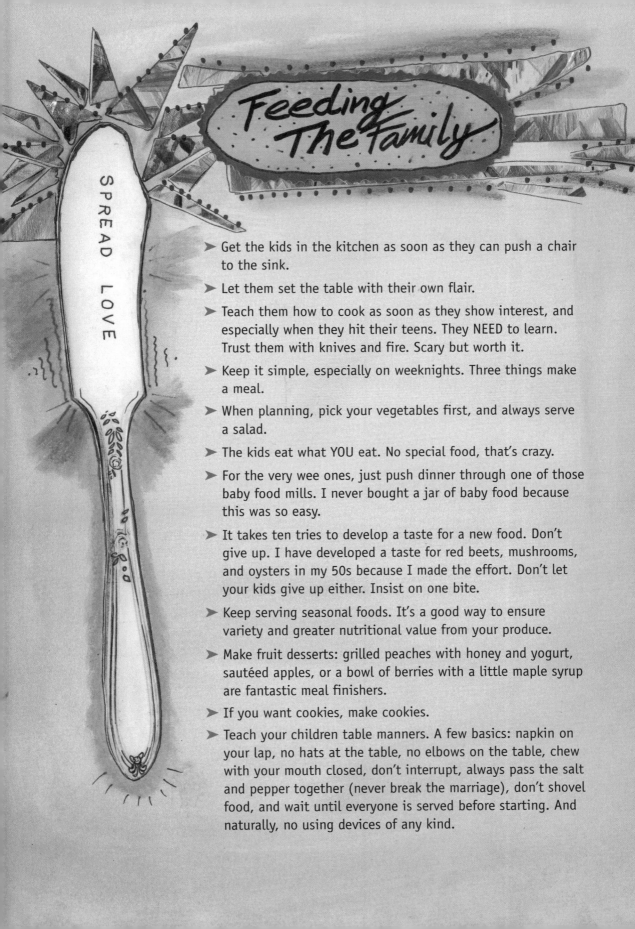

Feeding The Family

SPREAD LOVE

- ➤ Get the kids in the kitchen as soon as they can push a chair to the sink.

- ➤ Let them set the table with their own flair.

- ➤ Teach them how to cook as soon as they show interest, and especially when they hit their teens. They NEED to learn. Trust them with knives and fire. Scary but worth it.

- ➤ Keep it simple, especially on weeknights. Three things make a meal.

- ➤ When planning, pick your vegetables first, and always serve a salad.

- ➤ The kids eat what YOU eat. No special food, that's crazy.

- ➤ For the very wee ones, just push dinner through one of those baby food mills. I never bought a jar of baby food because this was so easy.

- ➤ It takes ten tries to develop a taste for a new food. Don't give up. I have developed a taste for red beets, mushrooms, and oysters in my 50s because I made the effort. Don't let your kids give up either. Insist on one bite.

- ➤ Keep serving seasonal foods. It's a good way to ensure variety and greater nutritional value from your produce.

- ➤ Make fruit desserts: grilled peaches with honey and yogurt, sautéed apples, or a bowl of berries with a little maple syrup are fantastic meal finishers.

- ➤ If you want cookies, make cookies.

- ➤ Teach your children table manners. A few basics: napkin on your lap, no hats at the table, no elbows on the table, chew with your mouth closed, don't interrupt, always pass the salt and pepper together (never break the marriage), don't shovel food, and wait until everyone is served before starting. And naturally, no using devices of any kind.

Be Not Simply Good Be Good for Something

CHAPTER TWO

Love in a Bowl

SOUP

THE STORY OF SOUP

When I was a mere twenty years old, I married the love of
my life, my Johnny. We spent our first five years in New
York City, where I became the best waitress in the world.
I loved it. I started at the Mad Hatter on the Upper East
Side, serving burgers, and ended at Covent Gardens, slicing
chateaubriand tableside. I loved being on the floor, but I
was mesmerized by the kitchen. One night I saw another
waitress, I'll call her Deana, smuggling duck carcasses out
of the restaurant. I asked her what was happening, and
she invited me over for breakfast the next morning to find
out. She showed me how to start a proper stock and fed me
homemade pumpkin pie and strong coffee. I was smitten.

Thus began my obsession with making stock. I procured
my own illegal duck carcasses, and for several weeks on my
day off, I would make the most delicious stock in all the
land. With Deana and the *The Joy of Cooking* as my coaches,
I taught myself how to build a rich, dark stock, and then,
because I could, I clarified it with egg shells. I made a stiff
aspic. I made a buttery consommé I can still taste. I was
enchanted by the kitchen chemistry in my hands. To this
day, I truly believe I am a soup master.

When I make a pot of soup, I pour my love into it. And
just like in *Like Water for Chocolate,* others feel the love and
are made happy, with full bellies, which helps them do what
we're meant to do: spread love. Another bonus—making
soup costs next to nothing. It's kitchen magic, and you can
make it happen.

PRACTICAL ADVICE FOR MAKING SOUP

The handiest pots and pans for soup making are a large, sturdy skillet and a five-quart stockpot with a reinforced bottom. Soups are best in big batches for sharing and leftovers; they always taste better when reheated after a day in the fridge. It's important not to skimp or get sloppy when prepping the vegetables. Cut them carefully by hand in intentional sizes. It adds more love to the end product, and it looks real pretty, too.

All good soups start with sautéing diced vegetables together for the first layer, most typically carrots, onion, celery, and garlic—this mixture is called a *mirepoix*. The measurements don't need to be exact. Feel free to improvise with additional herbs and such aromatics as ginger and garlic. Try adding extra ground spices when it suits your fancy. Fortify and layer your flavors by adding both dried and fresh herbs. Add a teaspoon of granulated garlic and onion when sautéing the garlic and onions. Ditto with fresh basil and dried basil, celery seed and celery, dried ginger and fresh ginger. Add roasted garlic to everything—it's always a delicious layer.

Don't hesitate to thin your soup the next day with water, stock, or milk. Add 1/4 cup at a time until you get your desired consistency. A dollop of yogurt, fresh herbs, vegan crema, crostini or croutons, or a drizzle of extra-green olive oil are all delicious toppers. I also recommend you finish every soup with a teaspoon each of vinegar and sugar. It enhances the flavor. But measure, please—don't ever pour vinegar directly into the pot. (Please learn from my mistakes.)

For an entrée, allow one and a half to two cups of soup per person. For a starter, one cup is usually plenty.

stock

Making homemade stock takes time. It makes great use of leftover meats, vegetable skins, and peelings, and the results are well worth the effort, but it's not a process that can be rushed. If you don't have that time, and you need some soup love, feel completely free to use store-bought stock or reconstituted powdered stock. I like vegetable stock as a rule, but feel free to experiment.

If you decide to make your own stock, I use the beef and chicken versions in *Mastering the Art of French Cooking* and the vegetable stock on TheKitchn.com.

HOW TO deglaze A PAN

Deglazing is a fun technique. Basically it's pouring cold wine, spirits, or stock into a hot pan to get up all the brown bits stuck to the bottom. Those brown bits, called "fond," are packed with flavor.

This is how it's done:
Pour off most of the fat in the pan. Turn the heat up to high. Swiftly, add cold liquid to the hot pan. Use a spatula or wooden spoon to scrape up the fond from the bottom and let it disperse into the liquid. Turn down the heat, simmer to reduce the liquid by about one-third, and then add it to the soup. Be careful when you deglaze with booze—it's flammable. But it's also really fun to play celebrity chef and burn off the liquor with dramatic flair. Be brave but be safe. Remove the pan from the heat when you add the spirits if fire scares you.

GRINDING whole SPICES

Cumin, coriander seeds, and cardamom are best ground right before use. A mortar and pestle are satisfying and efficient for this job, or a coffee grinder that's dedicated to grinding spices is also handy.

roasted garlic

If a recipe calls for garlic, summon your inner chef and add a layer of additional garlic flavor: Stir in the same amount of roasted garlic in addition to the fresh, adding it with the liquids. Here's how to roast garlic:

Preheat oven to 350°. Separate and peel a bulb of garlic. Arrange the cloves snugly in a single layer on a little pan with a high lip, like a small cake pan. Almost cover the garlic with equal parts water and olive oil, about 3 tablespoons each. A little bit of the cloves should be left uncovered. Bake until brown and soft, about 25 minutes. Shake pan halfway through cooking to rotate the garlic. Allow to cool and store in oil or purée it and keep in a clean jar in the refrigerator. I like to add a splash of coffee before roasting for color, as well as a few sprigs of thyme.

WHITE BEANS & GREENS SOUP

This is my favorite soup. Chef Ma made it twice a year when we had a ham, Easter and Christmas. She started with the hambone in a large pot of tap water and added ingredients all day. She still makes a heavenly ham-laden soup the day after our holidays. If you have a hambone, by all means drop it in. My recipe has more vegetables and greens, which make a colorful and fibrous addition.

Got rind? This is a great soup to drop a cheese rind (like parmesan) into. The rind will slowly melt away and add a layer of flavor. Larger rinds can be removed when the taste of the soup suits the chef.

Prep time: 30 minutes, plus overnight soaking
Cooking time: About 2 hours
Serves 8 to 12 (about 3 quarts)

1 pound dried white beans, picked over and soaked overnight in 4 quarts of
  water, then rinsed and drained
1 tablespoon plus 1 teaspoon cider or rice wine vinegar
4 sprigs fresh thyme or 1 teaspoon dried, divided
4 bay leaves, divided
6 cups vegetable stock
1 teaspoon celery seed
2 tablespoons olive oil
1 1/2 cups onion, diced
4 carrots, diced
6 cloves of garlic, minced
2 stalks celery, diced
1 cup white wine
2 cups tomato sauce (unseasoned) or diced tomatoes
1 bunch kale, cleaned and ripped into small pieces, ribs removed
1 teaspoon sugar
Sea salt and freshly ground pepper to taste

Place beans in large stockpot and cover with cold water by about 2 inches. Add 1 tablespoon vinegar, 2 sprigs or 1/2 teaspoon dried thyme, and 2 bay leaves. Bring to a boil. Lower to a simmer and cook until beans are soft, 30 to 60 minutes depending on the size of your beans (refer to the package directions). Pour into colander to drain, then return beans to stockpot. Add enough stock to cover, along with the remaining bay leaves, thyme, and celery seed, and return to a simmer.

Meanwhile, heat oil in large skillet and sauté the onion, carrots, garlic, and celery over medium-high heat until lightly browned, about 8 minutes. Add the mirepoix of vegetables to the stockpot. Deglaze the skillet with white wine, scraping up the bits from the bottom of the pan. Cook over medium-high heat until wine reduces by half, about 8 minutes; add to the stockpot along with tomatoes. Cover and simmer for 45 minutes. Add kale and cook another 10 minutes. Add 1 teaspoon each vinegar and sugar. Remove bay leaves and thyme sprigs. Add salt and pepper to taste.

Puree a portion of the soup or smash beans with a large spoon to thicken the soup, or leave it brothy if you prefer.

TOMATO BASIL SOUP WITH COCONUT MILK

Serve this soup with a peanut butter sandwich for a classic American lunch. The coconut milk is very subtle and good for you, too.

Prep time: 15 minutes
Cooking time: 45 to 50 minutes
Serves 6 to 8 (about 2 quarts)

2 tablespoons olive oil
2 carrots, finely chopped
1 large onion, finely chopped
4 cloves garlic, minced
1/4 cup flour
4 cups puréed or diced tomatoes (fresh or canned), with juice
Scant teaspoon baking soda (it acts as a stabilizer)
1 to 2 cups water
2 teaspoons dried basil
3 stalks fresh basil
1 14- to 16-ounce can coconut milk, light or regular
2 teaspoons sugar
2 teaspoons light-colored vinegar
1/2 teaspoon sea salt
1/2 teaspoon white pepper
Dash cayenne or other spicy pepper

In a stockpot, heat oil over medium heat and cook carrots, onion, and garlic until soft and translucent, about 7 minutes. Sprinkle flour on the vegetables and cook 3 minutes longer, slightly browning the flour. Working quickly, add the tomatoes, baking soda, and 1 cup water to the pot and stir. Bring to a boil, reduce heat to a simmer, and add herbs, coconut milk, sugar, vinegar, salt, pepper, and cayenne, stirring to combine. Simmer for 30 minutes, thinning with water if desired. Allow to cool slightly. Remove herb sprigs and purée the soup in batches, either in a blender or using an immersion blender, until smooth. Taste and add salt and pepper as needed.

tips for blending soup:

Blending hot soup can be life-threatening. Never ever put steaming hot soup in a blender and turn it on. It explodes from the 200°-plus heat and dangerous hot soup goes everywhere. Always let soup cool a bit, and fill the blender only half full. When it's time, put the lid on tightly, add a buffer of two tea towels, keep a hand firmly on top of the lid and towels, and start the blender on low. BE CAREFUL. Immersion blenders are safer for blending right in the soup pot, but you'll end up with a coarser finished product.

JC Says

Always use a bigger pot than you think you'll need.

cape verde vegetable soup

This is a brothy, satisfying soup with a kick. The ground coriander and orange zest add intrigue. Note that unlike with parsley, the stems of cilantro are not bitter, so you can chop them up with the leaves, no problem.

Prep time: 20 minutes
Cooking time: 40 minutes
Serves 8 to 12 (about 3 quarts)

3 tablespoons olive oil
2 celery stalks, diced
1 medium onion, finely chopped
2 carrots, diced
1 red or green bell pepper, diced
1 tablespoon minced ginger
4 garlic cloves, minced
1 teaspoon freshly ground coriander seeds
4 cups green cabbage, diced
5 red potatoes, diced into 3/4-inch cubes

2 cups diced tomatoes, fresh or canned, with juice
6 cups vegetable stock
1 teaspoon dried red chile flakes
1 tablespoon orange zest
1 teaspoon sugar
1 teaspoon light-colored vinegar
1/2 bunch cilantro, finely chopped
1 teaspoon sea salt

In a large soup pot, heat olive oil and sauté celery, onion, carrots, bell pepper, ginger, and garlic until lightly browned, about 8 minutes. Add ground coriander and sauté until the aroma starts releasing, about 1 more minute. Add cabbage, potatoes, tomatoes, and stock. Bring to boil on medium-high heat and reduce to simmer until potatoes are soft, about 30 minutes. Stir in red chile flakes, orange zest, sugar, vinegar, cilantro, and salt. Taste and add more salt and pepper if desired.

best ever lentil soup

This was my first ever original recipe. I still think it's one of the best lentil soups in the whole wide world. Simple and classic. It works with red, brown, or green lentils or a combination. The red lentils will melt into a purée, and the green ones will hold their shape. My favorites are the small green French ones.

TIP: Pick over all your legumes before soaking. Spread them out on a cookie sheet with a lip and give them a good once over, removing any little pebbles, odd chunks, or sticks.

Prep time: 30 minutes
Cooking time: 1 hour
Serves 8 to 12 (about 3 quarts)

2 tablespoons olive oil
1 cup finely chopped onion
4 cloves garlic, minced
1 cup finely chopped carrot
1 cup finely chopped celery
2 bay leaves
3 sprigs thyme
1/2 teaspoon freshly ground coriander
1 teaspoon celery seed
1 pound lentils, picked and rinsed

2 cups peeled and chopped tomatoes, fresh or canned
6 cups vegetable stock
1 cup thawed frozen corn puréed in 1 cup water
1 teaspoon sea salt
1 teaspoon freshly ground pepper
2 teaspoons balsamic vinegar
2 teaspoons sugar

Heat olive oil in a soup pot and sauté onion, carrots, celery, garlic, bay leaves, thyme, coriander, and celery seed over medium heat until onions are soft and translucent, about 6 minutes. Add lentils, tomatoes, and broth and stir to combine. Increase heat to high and bring just to a boil. Reduce heat to low and simmer until lentils are tender, approximately 45 minutes, scraping the bottom of the pan with a wooden spoon in 10-minute intervals. Add corn purée and stir. Add salt, pepper, vinegar, and sugar. Taste and add more salt and pepper if desired.

This is a thick, chunky soup; if you want it creamier, remove 4 cups, puree in a blender, and return to soup pot.

Miso Mushroom Barley Soup

We all need more barley in our lives. It's easy, it's versatile, it's a nice alternative to rice as a side dish, and it makes a mighty fine soup. Like this one. If you soak the barley, it'll cook faster, and some say it's more nutritious. Warning: Miso is very salty. You might want to start by reducing the miso by half if you're salt sensitive. You can always add more, but you can't take it out.

Prep time: 45 minutes
Cooking time: 50 minutes
Serves 10 (2 1/2 quarts)

3 tablespoons olive oil, divided
1/2 cup uncooked barley,
    soaked overnight if desired
6 cups water
1 teaspoon sea salt
1 yellow onion, diced
6 garlic cloves, minced
2 bay leaves
2 teaspoons chopped fresh
    rosemary
1/2 to 1 pound mushrooms (any
    combination), sliced or
    diced into bite-size pieces,
    including stems
2 celery stalks, diced
3 carrots, diced
3/4 cup sherry, Marsala,
    or red wine
1/3 cup white or yellow miso
1 teaspoon red wine vinegar
1 teaspoon sugar
1/2 teaspoon freshly ground
    pepper

If you soaked the barley, drain it (no need to dry it). Sauté barley in 1 tablespoon olive oil over medium heat until you can smell it toasting, about 2 minutes. Add to soup pot, stir in water and salt, cover, and bring to a boil.

While barley boils, sauté onion, rosemary, and bay leaves in remaining 2 tablespoons olive oil in a large skillet on medium-high heat until soft and translucent, about 6 minutes. Add garlic and sauté until lightly browned, about 3 minutes. Add to the boiling barley in the soup pot. Sauté mushrooms in same pan over medium-high heat and add to pot when they start to brown. Add celery and carrots to the soup pot and reduce heat to simmer. Deglaze the sauté pan with wine, scraping up any tasty bits on the bottom. Cook over medium-high heat until reduced by half, about 8 minutes, and add to pot. If the barley was soaked, it should be soft and ready. If it was not soaked, continue simmering until soft, about another 20 minutes, scraping the bottom of the pot to avoid sticking after 10 minutes. Remove pot from heat.

In a small bowl, whisk together miso and a scoop of liquid from the stockpot. When smooth, add back to the stockpot, with vinegar, sugar, and pepper. Stir, taste, and add salt and/or pepper if desired, keeping in mind that miso is salty!

Miso is fermented bean paste. It takes about a year to make, and it's full of beneficial enzymes and other amazing health attributes—as long as you don't boil it; it's best to add it to a soup after it has been removed from direct heat. To avoid lumps, first thin the miso in a small bowl and break up lumps with a whisk. Or melt it through a sieve directly into the soup. Don't worry if the soup boils and you kill the miso. It'll still be delicious, just not as full of those good enzymes.

Always use a wine in your cooking that you would want to drink, for obvious reasons...it'll taste better! Except for Marsala, which lends a smokiness and a little age. Marsala and sherry are both cheap, predictable, and delicious in soups and sauces. Refrigerate all wines after opening to extend their shelf lives.

albondigas soup

This California favorite is a time-consuming endeavor, but it's worth the effort. It's a classic Mexican soup with little rice-studded meatballs in a vegetable-rich broth. If you prefer ground turkey, use a blend of light and dark meat for juicer meatballs.

Prep time: About 45 minutes
Cooking time: About 45 minutes
Serves 12 or more (about 3 quarts)

meatballs

1 pound ground beef or turkey
1/2 cup coarsely grated zucchini
1/4 cup finely grated onion (use a cheese grater)
2 tablespoons breadcrumbs
1 large egg, beaten
1/3 cup uncooked white rice
2 tablespoons minced mint
2 tablespoons minced cilantro
2 garlic cloves, minced
1 tablespoon ground cumin
1 teaspoon dried, crumbled oregano (Mexican if you have it)
1/2 teaspoon sea salt
1/2 teaspoon red pepper

Combine all ingredients in a mixing bowl and knead gently to combine. Roll into little meatballs that will fit on a soup spoon, about 3/4 inch in diameter, about 40. Place on a cookie sheet and chill while preparing the soup base.

soup base

3 tablespoons olive oil
1 onion, finely diced
3 garlic cloves, minced
2 quarts chicken, beef, or vegetable stock
1 cup jarred or canned tomato sauce or diced tomatoes in juice
1/2 pound green beans, cut into 1-inch pieces
2 carrots, peeled and sliced into coins
1 teaspoon dried crumbled oregano (Mexican if you have it)
1 1/2 cups frozen or fresh green peas
1 tablespoon fresh lime or lemon juice
1 teaspoon sugar
1 teaspoon light-colored vinegar
Sea salt and freshly ground pepper to taste
1/2 cup chopped cilantro
Tortilla strips for garnish

Heat oil in large stockpot and sauté onions and garlic over medium heat until lightly browned, about 8 minutes. Add stock, tomatoes, green beans, carrots, and oregano. Increase heat to high and bring to a boil, then reduce heat to simmer. Gently add chilled, raw meatballs to the soup. Cover and let simmer undisturbed for 25 minutes. Add peas and simmer 5 more minutes. Add lemon or lime juice, sugar, and vinegar. Taste and adjust salt and pepper as needed.

Garnish with tortilla strips and cilantro.

A LITTLE TIP
Another way to fortify the flavor of your soup
if it's a little flat is to add a bouillon cube.

ZUPPA PASTA FAGIOLE

Sometimes I crave pasta fagiole. It harkens back to my navy bean childhood. This is a quick soup that makes me really happy. It's vegetarian; if you don't serve with Parmesan, it's vegan, and if you add a little sausage or bacon, I won't tell anyone.

Prep time: 15 minutes
Cooking time: About 35 minutes
Serves 8 to 12 (about 3 quarts)

2 tablespoons olive oil
1 teaspoon chopped rosemary
1/2 teaspoon dried thyme or 2 sprigs fresh thyme
2 bay leaves
1 medium onion, finely chopped
1 small carrot, finely chopped
1 rib celery, finely chopped
4 large cloves garlic, minced
1/2 teaspoon sea salt
1/2 teaspoon white pepper
1 cup canned crushed tomatoes (optional)
4 cups water
3/4 cup orzo, uncooked
1 1/2 cups cooked white beans (or 1 15-ounce can, rinsed and drained)
3 tablespoons roasted garlic
1 cup white wine
1 15-ounce can refried vegetarian beans
1 teaspoon sugar
1 teaspoon light-colored vinegar
Grated parmesan

Place a large soup pot over medium-high heat and add oil. Add herbs, bay leaves, chopped vegetables, and fresh garlic. Sauté until vegetables are soft, about 6 minutes. Season with salt and pepper. Add tomatoes, water, and orzo and boil until the pasta is soft, about 5 minutes. Add beans, roasted garlic, and wine. Reduce heat to medium and cook soup, scraping the bottom of the pot every 5 minutes, for about 20 minutes. Add sugar and vinegar, taste, and adjust salt and pepper as needed.

Serve topped with freshly grated parmesan.

VARIATION: Add 1/2 pound crumbled uncooked sausage or diced bacon when sautéing the vegetables.

TIP: Keep stirring and scraping the bottom of the pot while the soup cooks. If you scorch the bottom of the pot and burn the soup, there is no remedy—you'll have to throw it out. I know it's harsh, but it's the sad, sad truth. You'll know because of the burnt smell, a smell that forever haunts me in my professional kitchen. If you act fast and don't scrape up the burned bits from the bottom, sometimes you can pour off the top part before the burned flavor permeates the body of the soup. Act swiftly if this happens to you.

LOVE IN A BOWL: SOUP

Sunshine GINGER SOUP

For our purposes, let's remember that a pumpkin is a winter squash and works great in this recipe. This is the soup we Angelenos start craving and all the restaurants serve when the Los Angeles weather dips below 60 degrees—we call it "winter."

Prep time: 15 minutes, plus more if you roast the squash
Cooking time: About 1 hour
Serves 6 to 8 (about 2 quarts)

3 tablespoons olive oil
1 pound winter squash or carrots, or any combination thereof
1 onion, finely chopped
4 garlic cloves, minced
4 tablespoons minced ginger
1 teaspoon dried ginger
1 cinnamon stick
2 sprigs fresh thyme or 1/2 teaspoon dried thyme
1/2 teaspoon ground cumin
Dash cayenne pepper
4 cups stock or water
1 15.5-ounce can coconut milk
Juice of 1/2 lemon
Juice of 1/2 orange
1 tablespoon orange zest
1 teaspoon real maple syrup
1 teaspoon light-colored vinegar
Sea salt and freshly ground pepper to taste

Peel squash with a vegetable peeler, remove seeds, and slice into large chunks, as if you're making mashed potatoes, and set aside.

Place large stockpot over medium heat, add oil, and sauté onions, garlic, fresh ginger, dried ginger, cinnamon stick, thyme, cumin and cayenne until translucent, about 6 minutes. Add squash and stock or water, bring to a boil, reduce heat to medium-low, and cook until vegetables are super soft, about 30 minutes. Add coconut milk, lemon juice, orange juice, zest, maple syrup, and vinegar. Stir and mash the squash and cook for an additional 10 minutes. Add more stock or water if necessary to achieve the consistency you prefer. Allow to cool slightly, remove the cinnamon stick and thyme sprigs, and purée in a blender or with an immersion blender. Taste and add salt and pepper if necessary.

VARIATION:
Add a tablespoon of curry powder
when sautéing the onion.

BEST PARTY EVER

Every Fourth of July on the homestead, our family had a huge holiday barbecue. Practically the entire town and surrounding rural areas were in attendance. Chef Ma carefully orchestrated the menu, and every invitation had a handwritten "ask" on it, so she could have the correct quantities of potato salad, slaw, cupcakes, baked beans, and watermelon. We provided the burgers and dogs, kegs of beer and root beer, snow cones, and fireworks. The wee ones crafted ice into snow cones with old-fashioned ice scrapers. The men dressed in white short shorts and played volleyball and horseshoes. After-dinner relays included three-legged races and a rousing peanut scramble. There were prizes. Chef Ma wore a floor-length apron and stuffed its rows of pockets with bubble gum and diamond rings for the winning teams. When the sun finally set and the lightning bugs appeared, it was time for fireworks. Illegally purchased and launched from the far side of the pool by Pa and my brothers, it was the highlight of the night. Soon the crowd, a little boozy, well fed and played, would raise their voices and croon a heartfelt rendition of "God Bless America." Best. Fourth. Ever.

Chef Ma ran that party like a pro. To do that same party today, my best advice would be to hire a caterer, and I'm not just saying that because I'm a caterer. We come in, we set up, we tend to your guests, your bar, and your buffet, and then we slice the cake and quietly exit, leaving no trace behind, and you get to enjoy the party and be fully functional the next day.

If hired help is not an option, then make sure to plan ahead and ask for help. When friends ask what can they do, give them a job! Many hands make light work. Throwing a party for fifty to a hundred guests takes time management, logistics, and communication. Line everything up, and you could actually enjoy the party, too.

THROWING A BIG PARTY

INVITATIONS: Send invitations or e-vites at least four weeks in advance. Six weeks is better. Don't hesitate to call guests who haven't responded in a timely manner. An accurate head count brings peace of mind.

RENTALS: Arrange your furniture rentals and other needs at least three weeks in advance. Get rentals delivered the day before and picked up the day after, or borrow stuff. Parties need tables, chairs, tablecloths, glasses, plates, cutlery, and napkins. Check your order on arrival to make sure it's complete.

PAPER PRODUCTS: Allow 1.5 plates per guest, two or three glasses, three beverage napkins, and two dinner napkins. For cutlery, allow a twenty percent overage, and don't forget to add more for dessert and appetizers.

FOOD AND MENU: Plan the menu as soon as you decide to have a party. If you're cooking all by yourself (so sad), take advantage of that modern miracle, the freezer, and make desserts, soups, stews, or casseroles weeks in advance. Label and date everything. Place an order with your local establishments and confirm three days prior. Or be like Chef Ma and make a coordinated potluck—assign specific dishes and quantities. It's a great model!

BEVERAGES: Serve elixirs in two-gallon vessels with lots of ice and fresh fruit and forgo individual beverages. You can make one boozy and another nonalcoholic. Say no to soda. If you feel the need to serve beer, a keg works better for a crowd than cans or bottles. And if you want to offer wine, set up a self-service table with pre-opened bottles (put the white on ice) and plenty of glasses. If you're serving booze, serve coffee, too.

MUSICA!: Book your musician buddies at least a month before the event. Or create a playlist when you're relaxed and feeling festive—anytime but the day of the event.

DECOR & PARTY FAVORS: Get some flowers from the farmers' market, stuff them in jars and vases, and place them everywhere. Light lots of five-hour votive candles before the guests come. Little pots of herbs, strands of ivy, or branches from the garden are excellent buffet adornments. Finally, it's nice (but by no means essential) to offer a little party favor. I like to send guests home with a cookie or a breakfast muffin for the next morning.

TABLE COVERINGS: Dress your tables properly for a celebration, even if it's butcher paper and crayons—it's important for the ambience. I recommend hitting the fabric stores for prints, textures, and lots of yardage.

SERVING EQUIPMENT: Every dish needs a serving platter and utensil. Do the math and see what you have. I've found fun pieces at thrift stores, restaurant supply houses, and the 99 Cent store.

SETTING THE BUFFET: Make sure the table is protected if it's fancy—newspaper or old blankets work under tablecloths in a pinch. Put the forks and knives at the end of the buffet or on the side, so people don't have to juggle them while loading their plates. Always start with the big foods that fill up the plate, like bread and salad, and put the entrées as the last item.

PHOTOGRAPHS: Ask a friend to take pictures. Then it's off your plate.

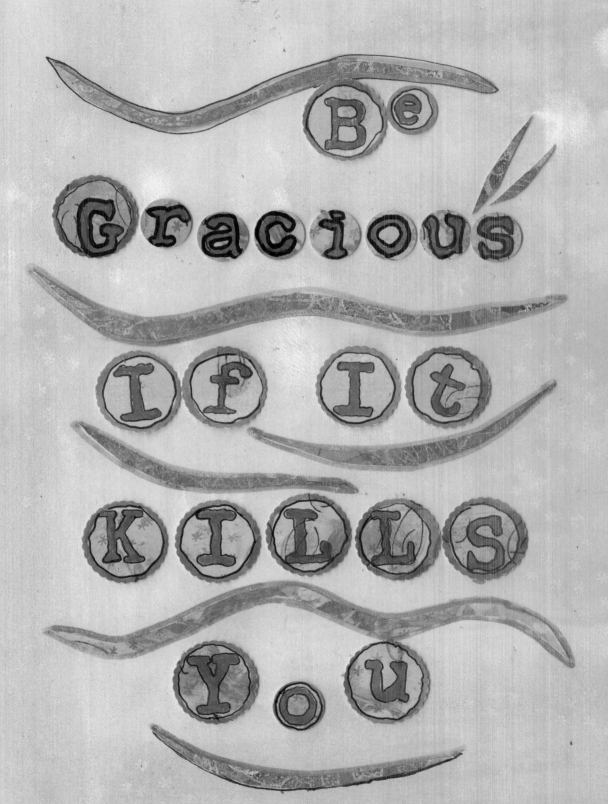

Chapter Three
Catering Classics

Welcome to California

When I moved to California in the spring of 1984, I was immediately enchanted. I stayed in a darling Spanish bungalow with my friend Chris from acting school. He lived in Beachwood Canyon under the Hollywood sign, where the palm trees swayed as if on cue, and hummingbirds visited my window every morning. My sense of belonging in California was unquestionable. I was ready to put down roots.

I got a job at another burger joint, Hampton's in Hollywood, and met my first business partner, Kathy. She was a stand-in actress for game shows, and she baked desserts for Hampton's. She often took her treats to work on the game show, and one day the producer said, "Hey, you wanna cater?" She said, "Sure!" and asked me to join her. Baker and Cook Catering Company was hatched in the spring of 1985. We'd split the menu in half and meet at the site, having prepared all the food in our separate apartments. It was a little illegal. But we set a beautiful table and made friends with the crew members, taking their requests and serving a lot of fruit crumble. It was a great job. Kathy and I worked together for two years, then split up the pots and pans and went our separate ways. I kept cooking, with a baby on each hip.

In 1987, Johnny and I bought a cute corner house in Echo Park. The kids ran wild, barefoot, and dirty, seemingly in the center of Los Angeles, and I ran my catering company from the rickety kitchen for six years. These were the best of times.

I'll admit that I'm sharing these classic recipes from my catering business reluctantly, because now you'll all know how easy my job is.

 A word on Seafood

The more I know about seafood, the less I want to eat it, and the less I want you to eat it. Not because I don't love it, because I do, I love it all, and I know how much you do, too. But we need to pay more attention to where our food comes from, and we definitely need to protect and restore our oceans. What would we do without the blue part of our planet?

If you love seafood, that's great—just ask questions about where your fish is from and support local vendors who use sustainable fishing or fish-farming practices. Do it for our beautiful beaches and for the future generations who will rely on the planet's oceans for livelihood and continued pleasure. Practice moderation, explore lesser-known varieties, and make conscious choices.

I'm a fan of Loch Duarte Sustainable Salmon farms in Scotland, but then I think, "What about the carbon footprint of getting it to Los Angeles?" It's all a balancing act. Awareness and education will help us get where we need to be—and we'll do it together.

 SASSY 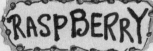 RASPBERRY  SALMON

This quick and easy salmon recipe is a bizarre combination of strong flavors that blend together into tantalizing flavor. It's absolutely sassy next to the Amazing Corn Sensation on page 85.

Prep time: 10 minutes
Cooking time: 8 minutes
Serves 4 to 6

1/2 cup raspberry jam
1 heaping teaspoon chile garlic sauce
  (Huy Fong brand is standard)
1 tablespoon chopped cilantro
1 heaping teaspoon prepared horseradish

2 teaspoons or so fresh lemon juice
1 pound salmon fillet cut into
  4 to 6 pieces
2 teaspoons olive oil
Sea salt and fresh pepper to taste

Preheat broiler. In a small bowl, mix jam, chile garlic, cilantro, horseradish, and lemon juice and combine well. Set aside.

Rub salmon with olive oil and sprinkle with salt and pepper. Place skin side down on a baking sheet lined with foil. Broil for 4 minutes. Top with the glaze and broil until the fish is flaky and the sauce is bubbling, about 4 more minutes.

exotic salad

You have to try this salad—it's so easy and so good. Keep in mind that I drink salad dressing, so you should start with less dressing than I suggest, unless you drink salad dressing, too.

Prep time: 5 minutes, plus more to make dressing
Serves 3 to 4

6 cups mixed greens
2 to 3 tablespoons Balsamic Vinaigrette (*see recipe next page*)
1/2 cup toasted walnuts
10 dried apricots cut into 1/4-inch-thick slices
1/4 cup crumbled feta or goat cheese

Toss the greens with 2 tablespoons of vinaigrette; taste and add more dressing if you like. Place greens on a platter, arrange apricots and nuts on the greens, and top with the cheese of your choice.

balsamic vinaigrette

Salad dressings last forever in the refrigerator, if they're kept in a clean, well-sealed jar. Use this terrific vinaigrette as a base for all your dressings and marinades. I could drink this dressing. In fact, I have.

Prep time: 10 minutes
Makes about 3 1/2 cups

1 cup cider vinegar
1/3 cup balsamic vinegar
1 tablespoon Dijon mustard
1 teaspoon dried Italian herb blend
2 garlic cloves
1/4 cup roughly chopped red onion
1 to 2 cups olive oil
1 teaspoon sea salt
1/2 teaspoon freshly ground pepper

Combine vinegars, mustard, herbs, garlic, and onion in a blender. Cover and blend until smooth. With the motor running, drizzle in 1 cup olive oil in a slow, steady stream until emulsified. Taste and blend in more oil, slowly, as you prefer. I like my dressings real tangy, so I use less oil.

CURRIED CAULIFLOWER SALAD

Eat more cauliflower! This recipe will make it easy—it really pops with flavor. This is a great dish to bring to a potluck.

Prep time: 20 minutes
Cooking time: 15 to 20 minutes
Serves 6 to 10

1/4 cup plus 2 tablespoons olive oil
2 tablespoons curry powder
1 teaspoon sea salt, divided
1/4 teaspoon freshly ground cumin
1/4 teaspoon ground coriander
1 tablespoon grated or minced ginger
1 head cauliflower, broken or cut into florets
2 tablespoons maple syrup
3 tablespoons fresh lemon juice
1/4 teaspoon freshly ground pepper

6 dried apricots, diced
1/4 cup dried currants
1/4 cup diced red or green onion
1 red pepper, seeded and diced
1/2 cup raw or roasted cashews
    or sliced almonds
1/4 bunch chopped cilantro

Preheat oven to 425°. In a large bowl, whisk together 2 tablespoons olive oil, curry powder, 1/2 teaspoon salt, cumin, coriander, and ginger. Add cauliflower florets and toss, evenly coating the cauliflower. Spread the florets in a single layer on a baking sheet and roast until lightly browned and cooked through, checking at 10 and 15 minutes, about 20 minutes total. Remove from oven and let cool.

While cooling, prepare the dressing. In a small bowl, whisk together the maple syrup, lemon juice, 1/4 cup olive oil, 1/2 teaspoon salt, and pepper. Set aside.

When cauliflower is cool enough to handle, add apricots, currants, onion, pepper, nuts, and cilantro. Add dressing and toss to coat everything. Taste and add salt and pepper if desired.

VARIATION:
Add some chickpeas for additional nutrition.

CUMIN SCENTED TURKEY MEATLOAF

Pa didn't like meatloaf, so we never ate it growing up. I, however, love it so much that I could eat it twice a week. This is not your typical grainy meatloaf—the oats create an almost creamy center. It also makes a killer sandwich the next day, with some Pommery mustard and sliced tomatoes. Try to avoid supermarket ground turkey—it'll taste better if it comes from a butcher, rancher, or other quality source.

Prep time: 30 minutes
Cooking time: 1 1/4 to 1 1/2 hours
Makes 1 to 2 loaves, serving about 10

2 tablespoons olive oil
1 stalk celery, finely diced
1/2 yellow onion, finely diced
   (mince other half to use in Creamy Gravy)
2 carrots, finely diced
3 cloves garlic, minced
1 pound ground turkey (mix of white and
   dark meat)
1 teaspoon salt

1 teaspoon freshly ground pepper
1/2 teaspoon cayenne
1 teaspoon ground cumin
1 egg, beaten
1/4 cup ketchup
1/4 cup milk (any variety)
1/3 cup breadcrumbs
3/4 cup quick oats
Extra ketchup and onion slices

Preheat oven to 350°. In a medium sauté pan, heat olive oil and sauté celery, 1/2 onion, carrots, and garlic until soft and slightly browned, about 10 minutes. Set aside to cool.

Meanwhile, in a large bowl combine turkey, salt, pepper, cayenne, cumin, egg, ketchup, milk, breadcrumbs, and oats and mix well. Add the cooled mirepoix and mix again. Form into 1 or 2 free-form meatloaves. Alternatively, smash flat in a 9" x 9" pan, like a pan of brownies. Cover with foil and bake for 30 minutes. Remove foil. Brush a thin coat of ketchup on top of the meat and garnish with a few raw onion slices. Return to oven and bake until brown, another 30 to 45 minutes. An internal meat thermometer should reach 160 degrees in the very center of the loaf. Serve with Creamy Gravy (next page).

CREAMY GRAVY

Prep time: 5 minutes
Cooking time: 15 minutes
Makes about 3 cups

1/2 onion, minced
3 tablespoons olive oil
2 tablespoons flour
2 cups stock (chicken or vegetarian)
1 tablespoon ketchup
1 to 2 teaspoons soy sauce
1/4 cup milk (any variety)

In a medium sauté pan, heat oil on high and sauté onion until slightly brown, about 8 minutes. Reduce heat to medium, add flour, and cook, stirring, to brown the flour, an additional 1 to 2 minutes. Slowly whisk in stock and allow gravy to come to a boil, stirring constantly. Add ketchup, 1 teaspoon soy sauce, and milk and reduce heat to a simmer. Taste and add more soy sauce or ketchup if desired. Strain out the onions if you like a smooth gravy. Serve in an adorable gravy boat next to your meatloaf, or with any roast meat or fritters.

MY FRIEND KETCHUP

Ketchup: It's my secret ingredient. Stir some up with soy and ginger for a quick barbecue sauce. Add a spoonful or two to your béchamel for mac 'n' cheese, and add it to the gravies in this book for a little extra color and piquant sweetness.

Silver Palate Party Chicken

Sometime in the early 1980s, I got a book that changed my life. So did two million other folks. It was called *The Silver Palate Cookbook*, and authors Sheila Lukins and Julee Rosso made cooking fun, interesting, and accessible. This is an ode to their Chicken Marbella, a caterer's dream of an entrée. The baked dried fruits are sublime with the succulent, marinated, slightly sweet chicken. Thank you, ladies, for cooking with love, and for inspiring me.

Prep time: 15 minutes plus overnight marinating
Cooking time: 50 minutes to 1 hour

1 chicken, 3 to 4 pounds, quartered
6 cloves garlic, minced
1 teaspoon dried thyme or 4 sprigs fresh
1 teaspoon sea salt
1 teaspoon freshly ground pepper
1/4 cup cider vinegar
1/4 cup olive oil
10 pitted prunes

20 pitted green olives
10 dried apricots
3 bay leaves
1 orange, skin on, thinly sliced
1/4 cup brown sugar
Scant 1/4 cup white wine
1/4 cup chopped cilantro or
      parsley, for garnish

In a large bowl, combine chicken quarters, garlic, thyme, salt, pepper, vinegar, olive oil, prunes, olives, apricots, and bay leaves. Cover and let marinate overnight in the refrigerator.

The next day, preheat oven to 350°. Line the bottom of a 9" x 13" baking pan with sliced oranges. Remove chicken from marinade and arrange atop the oranges with the dried fruits and olives. Pour enough marinade into the pan to cover the bottom with 1/4 inch of liquid.

Roast for 30 minutes uncovered. Sprinkle chicken pieces with brown sugar and douse with white wine, then roast until golden brown, an additional 20 to 30 minutes.

Serve with the baked fruits and olives spooned on top. Sprinkle generously with parsley or cilantro. Serve with couscous, barley, or rice to soak up the juices.

Honey Roasted Carrots

Prep time: 5 minutes (No chopping, no peeling!)
Cooking time: 50 minutes
Serves 2 to 4

2 teaspoons chile powder
1 teaspoon sea salt
1 teaspoon paprika (any kind)
2 tablespoons olive oil
2 tablespoons honey or maple syrup
1/4 cup water
1 pound unpeeled carrots, scrubbed and green tops removed

Preheat oven to 350°. In a small bowl, stir together chile powder, salt, paprika, olive oil, honey, and water. Lay whole carrots on a rimmed baking sheet and pour the sauce over them.

Roll the carrots around to coat. Roast for 30 minutes, then rotate the pan and shake the carrots so they roll to a different side. Roast for another 20 minutes. The carrots will shrivel and be very soft, toasty brown, and delicious.

GREEN BEANS with CHILE PECANS and SESAME DRESSING

This is an amazing and beautiful addition to any buffet and a treasure at a potluck. I love a good potluck, but they tend to be light on natural fiber. Back in the day, I would always try to bring something healthy like this to a potluck, along with any leftovers I had from the catering company. The dads loved to see me coming. I've always been popular with the dads who like to eat.

Note that you can prepare all the ingredients in advance and assemble the dish just before serving.

Prep time: 5 minutes, plus Sesame Dressing
Cooking time: 4 to 10 minutes, plus Chile Pecans
Serves 3 to 5

1 pound green beans, trimmed
1/2 cup Sesame Dressing (*see recipe page 82*)
1 cup Chile Pecans (*see recipe page 83*)
Sesame seeds for garnish

Blanch green beans in simmering salted water until crisp-tender, 6 to 10 minutes. Alternatively, you can steam green beans for 4 to 8 minutes. Test beans for doneness halfway through cooking time. When they're tender, shock beans to stop the cooking process by plunging them in cold water. Dry them and platter them or store in the refrigerator to use later.

When you're ready to eat, arrange cooked green beans on a pretty serving platter. Top with Sesame Dressing and Chile Pecans. Sprinkle with sesame seeds and serve.

SESAME DRESSING

This is super easy to mix—try using an old condiment jar. It'll separate as it sits, so shake it up to blend before serving.

Prep time: 10 minutes
Makes about 2 cups

3/4 cup olive or grapeseed oil
3/4 cup rice or cider vinegar
2 tablespoons soy sauce
2 teaspoons sugar
1/4 cup dark sesame oil

2 teaspoons Dijon mustard
1 clove garlic, minced
2 teaspoons minced ginger
1 teaspoon hot sauce

Combine all the ingredients in a 16- to 24-ounce jar with a tight-fitting lid. Shake to blend. Allow to mellow on the kitchen counter before use.

CHILE PECANS

Cooking time: 10 minutes
Makes 2 cups

2 cups pecan halves (walnuts also work)
1 tablespoon olive oil
1/4 cup brown sugar
1 teaspoon cayenne
1/4 cup water
1/8 teaspoon sea salt

Preheat oven to 350°. In a mixing bowl, stir together nuts, oil, brown sugar, cayenne, water, and salt, coating the nuts thoroughly. Spread nuts on a greased baking sheet with a lip, in a single layer. Roast until the sugar starts to bubble and nuts brown slightly, 8 to 10 minutes. Be sure to check at the halfway point and stir them if the edges are browning. Allow to cool and loosen with a spatula. Store in an airtight container. Do not refrigerate.

TOASTING WALNUTS

Sure, you can buy toasted walnuts, but they taste better when you do it yourself.

2 tablespoons olive oil
1 cup walnuts
Sea salt to taste

Heat olive oil in a 10-inch heavy skillet over moderate heat until hot but not smoking. Add nuts and sauté, stirring almost constantly, until golden, about 2 minutes. Do not walk away from the pan—once they're done they burn very quickly! When done, remove from heat and pour through a strainer to drain the oil. Transfer nuts to a plate and sprinkle with salt.

Roasting in the oven is also an option and is less stressful; see the Chile Pecan recipe above for the technique.

FARRO AL FRESCO

A little cup of grains goes a long way. This farro pilaf is equally appealing when made with quinoa, basmati rice, or couscous. Switch up the dried fruit for fresh apples or pears, change the spinach to arugula, and try another kind of cheese, and you'll have an entirely different dish. Try new things. Deliciousness is waiting for you.

Prep time: 20 minutes
Cooking time: 10 to 30 minutes for the farro, depending on the type
Serves 4 to 6

1 cup farro, cooked in salted water according to package directions
1 cup spinach chiffonade*
1/4 cup toasted almonds
1/4 cup dried fruit (such as currants, cranberries, figs, or apricots)
1/2 cup crumbled chèvre or feta
3 tablespoons Balsamic Vinaigrette (*see recipe page 73*)

Spread cooked farro on a cookie sheet and allow to cool. In a large bowl, add farro, spinach, almonds, and currants and toss. Arrange on a platter, top with crumbled cheese, and drizzle Balsamic Vinaigrette over all.

* chiffonade = cut into slivers

ALERT!
If you're making it ahead,
do not add the cheese and vinaigrette until serving time,
and heat the farro in the oven just enough
to take the chill off and soften the kernels.

My complicated relationship with Corn

As much as I've loved corn my whole life, I think our days together are numbered. The GMO thing is more than distressing, and when you get down to it, corn is what ranchers feed cows to get them fat. Do we really need to eat that, too, or should we leave it for the cows? That said, I still love it and continue to eat it in moderation.

When you're shopping to make the corn dish below, I recommend you buy the smallest container of masa you can find, or you'll be making tortillas and tamales and pupusas and sopes forever. (Give them a Google and get busy with all that extra harina!)

the Amazing Corn Sensation

I developed this simple, old-fashioned corn pudding for the line producer on *Seinfeld*. She was missing her mama's corn pudding and asked if I could make her one for a crew meal. Voilà! Corn pudding So Cal style. The masa gives it a really nice tamale flavor, and the cheddar works perfectly. It earns its name every time it is served.

Prep time: 15 minutes
Cooking time: 45 minutes
Serves 6 to 8

1 1/2 cups milk (any kind)
2 tablespoons olive or grapeseed oil
3 cups thawed frozen corn
2 eggs

1 tablespoon honey or sugar
1/4 cup masa (corn flour)
1 1/2 teaspoons sea salt
1 cup grated cheddar

Preheat oven to 350°. In a blender, combine milk, oil, and 2 1/2 cups corn and puree until almost smooth. Add eggs, honey or sugar, masa, and salt and blend until combined. Pour into greased 9" x 9" baking dish or pie plate. Bake until fork comes out clean, about 45 minutes. Sprinkle with cheddar and remaining 1/2 cup corn and bake until cheese is melted, only about 5 minutes.

Cinnamon Fruit Crumble

This is a great dessert that serves a crowd. The ingredients are kitchen staples, it cooks in a jiffy, and it's particularly fantastic with a mix of stone fruits and berries. There was a time when every job at Jennie Cooks had a fruit crumble with fresh cream for dessert. Why? Because people never get tired of it. There's always room for a little fruit and cream.

Prep time: 20 minutes
Cooking time: 40 minutes
Serves 8 to 10

6 cups fresh fruit in any combination, peeled and cut into chunks or slices as needed
3/4 cup sugar (or less)
1 teaspoon fresh lemon juice
2 tablespoons flour
1 tablespoon cinnamon

Crumb topping
1 cup all-purpose flour
1/2 cup quick oats
3/4 cup brown sugar
1/2 cup white sugar
1 tablespoon cinnamon
1 teaspoon baking powder
1 tablespoon vanilla extract
1 egg
3 tablespoons oil or melted butter, plus more for drizzling

Preheat the oven to 350°. Grease a 9" x 13" glass or ceramic baking pan or collect eight 8-ounce Ball jars (no greasing needed) and set aside. In a large bowl, gently toss together fruit, half the sugar, lemon juice, flour, and cinnamon. Taste and if fruit is too tart, add more sugar. Spread mixture evenly in jars or in greased baking pan.

Place all the crumb topping ingredients in a medium bowl. Using your hands, a spoon, or a mixer, blend the ingredients until it starts to turn into crumbles. Top the fruit with the crumble mixture and drizzle on a bit more oil or melted butter on top of the crumbs. Bake until the crumble is golden brown and the fruit is bubbling on the side of the pan or jars, about 30 minutes for jars and 40 minutes for pan (regardless of fruit). Let rest 10 minutes before serving so it sets up nicely.

A WORD ABOUT APPETIZERS

It's appropriate and expected to have a little something out when guests arrive. It's inappropriate, however, to stress out about it. For our housewarming party in 1987, I over-planned the menu and was truly in the weeds. I had petite tarts, stuffed dates, meat on sticks, and dumplings. I practically threw food at the guests while trying to get it out in a timely fashion. Perhaps no one knew this at the time but me (I try to always look calm and collected), but it sure was a terrible way to entertain.

I'm a big fan of simple appetizers. Bread, pita, or crostini with spreads like hummus or bruschetta cover all types of eaters. And who doesn't love a pickle plate? Sliced apples, a bowl of tangerines, or cucumber spears with lemon and chiles are popular with the kids.

It's okay to buy stuff, too. Quality from-the-freezer spanakopita and vegetable dumplings always earn yummy noises.

And never, ever forget the power of the cheese and salumi plate. It's a perfect starter for omnivores. I love to tuck in dried apricots, dates, and olives, and my local market has more than forty varieties of salumi to keep it interesting. (I love L.A.) Serve smoked meats with a little whole-grain mustard. Quince paste (also called *membrillo*) adds a nice sweetness to a sharp cheddar, and a hearty dollop of homemade preserves on top of a triple crème is a special kind of heaven. My friend Kathleen dresses up a simple chèvre to the max. She covers it with chopped olives or minced sun-dried tomatoes (or both), drizzles it with balsamic vinegar, tops it with a basil chiffonade, and serves it with crostini. It's practically a meal.

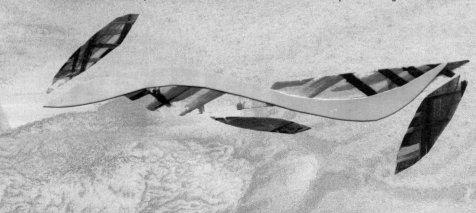

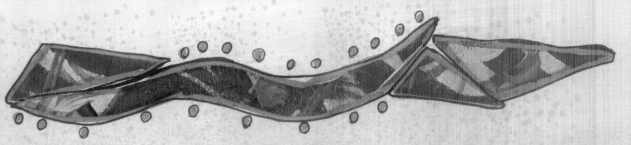

Great women have surrounded me all my life. My Nana was a badass. Rumor has it that she incinerated a mink stole she'd found, but we are never to speak of it. My Grammy was a pistol—I rubbed her bunions while watching *Gunsmoke* in her bed, eating vanilla wafers while she smoked Virginia Slims. You've come a long way, baby. My aunts were all beautiful women with big hearts, and they gave me lots of cousins. And Chef Ma always had a plethora of ladies running around, getting donations for the hospital, playing tennis, growing zucchini, making quilts, and sharing recipes. I had a constant supply of marshmallows in a cut-glass candy dish on the coffee table at Mrs. Fretz's house, and if we needed anything, I went down the hill to Mrs. Meinhold's corner store and walked it back up.

I know my success would not have been possible without the many women who have propped me up over the years. Many women chefs have moved through my kitchens. We keep in touch, but I hang my heart with the ladies from my current California family, the gals with whom I raised my now-twentysomething kids. They know me. They've been watching me for YEARS grow this crazy business into something I can be proud of. Through all the drama and milestones, we've grown into a thick posse of best friends. We've taken holidays together, shared many meals and celebrations, and blended our families so well that the kids all think they're blood relatives. We get together as often as we can when the kids are in town, and when they're not, we seize any excuse for a girls' night out.

I can speak for all my girlfriends when I say we love our family dinners in the kitchen. Usually, we're a crew of twenty to twenty-five. It's our time to be grateful for our families (and yes, of course, our husbands) and our friendships, and to come together in conviviality over wonderful food. We move the kitchen work tables outside and sit in the middle of the kitchen's scramble area, right in front of the ovens, bathed in the red hue of the party lights. We get a little boozy and laugh until our bellies hurt. I make sure the food is abundant, because you know what they say: "If there are no leftovers, then somebody's hungry." I create a balanced menu, because we have vegans and omnivores sitting elbow to elbow and I want everyone swooning over the food. We eat family style, passing courses up and down the table, and then we do it again so everybody can have seconds. At the end of the night, we stack the dishes in the sink, say our goodbyes, and kiss and hug with gusto. Girlfriends, mothers, and sisters—my better halves.

Chapter
Four
Mothers
and
Sisters

MOROCCAN LAMB TAGINE

When I was little, I hated lamb. Mostly I didn't like the way it smelled when it was roasting, and I didn't like the green jelly Chef Ma served with it. Fortunately, I grew up and gave it a second chance, and now, whaddya know, I like it! Lamb happens to be the favorite food of my friend Colleen, who's a food writer—and an unabashed picky eater. She hates ketchup, which is my favorite secret ingredient. She hates mayonnaise, and I want to marry it. And please, don't ever put cucumbers in her water. But oddly, she loves lamb, and I love her, therefore I try to serve lamb at our family suppers. I like it soft and stewed, I like it cut into little chops, and I love it ground as an alternative to beef. And to think it made me crazy as a child!

This recipe will make a lamb lover out of any doubters. It has a complex flavor that's heartwarming, unusual, and satisfying.

Prep time: 30 to 40 minutes
Cooking time: 2 1/2 to 3 hours
Serves 6 to 8

1 teaspoon cinnamon
1 teaspoon ground cumin
1 teaspoon ground ginger
1 teaspoon sea salt
1 teaspoon freshly ground pepper
2 pounds boneless lamb stew meat, cubed (I use the leg)
2 tablespoons olive oil
6 cloves garlic, minced
1 onion, finely diced
2 carrots, sliced into 1-inch coins
2 celery stalks, diced
1 teaspoon minced fresh ginger

1 bay leaf
1 28-ounce can chopped tomatoes, with juice
1 cup red wine
1 pinch saffron threads (optional)
2 3-inch cinnamon sticks
1 sweet potato, cut into pieces the same size as the carrots
1 can garbanzo beans, rinsed
2 teaspoons honey
Juice of 1/2 lemon (about 1 tablespoon)
Juice and zest of 1 orange
Chopped parsley for garnish

This may be cooked on the stovetop or in the oven. If you'd like to use the oven, preheat it to 350°.

In a large bowl, combine cinnamon, cumin, ginger, salt, and pepper. Add lamb and toss to coat. In a large skillet, heat olive oil over medium heat and sauté the pieces of lamb, in batches as necessary. When browned on all sides, transfer to a stockpot. Use the same skillet to sauté (stirring frequently) the garlic, onion, carrots, celery, and ginger until vegetables start to soften, about 5 minutes. Add softened vegetables, bay leaf, and tomatoes to the stockpot. Deglaze the skillet over high heat with the red wine, scraping up the tasty bits from the bottom of the pan. Add saffron and cinnamon sticks to the wine and boil for 5 minutes. Add wine mixture to the stockpot and turn heat to high. Bring liquid in the stockpot to a boil for 5 minutes, then reduce to a simmer and cook, covered, for 1 hour over low heat, or cook in oven for the same amount of time. Add sweet potatoes to pot, cover, and cook 1 more hour. The meat is done when it falls apart when pushed with a fork, so if it's not done yet, return to the heat or the oven for another 15 minutes and test again.

When the lamb is just falling apart, add garbanzos, honey, lemon juice, orange juice and zest, stir, and cook for 5 minutes. Taste and add salt and pepper if desired.

SWITCH:
This makes an equally spectacular chicken vindaloo—
just substitute chicken pieces for the lamb.

perfect roast chicken

My girlfriend Debra helped me raise my little ones and also to get my business on track before she moved back to the East Coast. We had a standing dinner with our little kids on Tuesday nights, and our menu was predictable: mac 'n' cheese, hot dogs, buttered peas, and (for the moms) white wine.

Debra's a vegetarian, but her family isn't. She called Chef Ma when her kids were little and asked for a roast chicken recipe. As far as I know, she's been roasting a chicken every week since. As a child, I didn't care if Chef Ma ever roasted chicken again. We ate it often, and I always got the undesirable breast meat, while my sibs hoarded the second joints and drumsticks. These days, I think roasted chicken is a perfect meal, especially when I get a thigh.

Chickens cook about 20 minutes per pound. Adjust your cooking time to suit the size of your bird. Better yet, get an instant-read thermometer and cook until the deepest part of the breast reads 160 degrees internally.

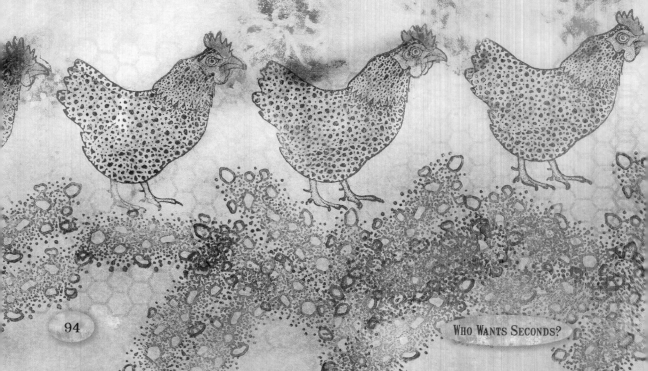

94

Prep time: 15 minutes
Cooking time: About 1 hour
Serves 4

2 tablespoons olive oil, divided
1 quality chicken (3 to 4 pounds), no fuss, no truss
1 pound carrots, unpeeled, cut in half
1 medium onion or fennel bulb, peeled and quartered
1 lemon, halved
1 tablespoon sea salt
1/2 teaspoon freshly ground pepper
6 sprigs thyme

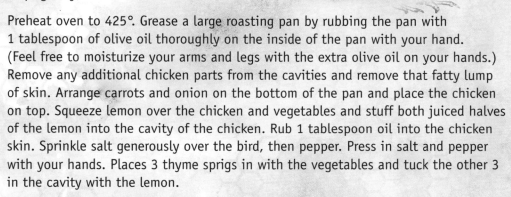

Preheat oven to 425°. Grease a large roasting pan by rubbing the pan with
1 tablespoon of olive oil thoroughly on the inside of the pan with your hand.
(Feel free to moisturize your arms and legs with the extra olive oil on your hands.)
Remove any additional chicken parts from the cavities and remove that fatty lump
of skin. Arrange carrots and onion on the bottom of the pan and place the chicken
on top. Squeeze lemon over the chicken and vegetables and stuff both juiced halves
of the lemon into the cavity of the chicken. Rub 1 tablespoon oil into the chicken
skin. Sprinkle salt generously over the bird, then pepper. Press in salt and pepper
with your hands. Places 3 thyme sprigs in with the vegetables and tuck the other 3
in the cavity with the lemon.

Roast for 20 minutes, reduce heat to 325°, and roast an additional 40 minutes.
Check internal temperature for doneness. Leave to rest for 10 minutes before cutting
so the juices settle into the meat. To cut, first remove the drumsticks and then the
thighs. Debone the breasts and serve them whole or cut into thirds. Platter the bird
with the carrots and onions and pour jus from the roasting pan on top.

Miriam's Lacquered Chicken

One of the first female chefs I ever hired was Chef Miriam. She was a petite woman who loved to cook and eat. She always had a new idea or a fresh recipe, and as I recall, she liked dirty jokes.

I've long noticed a funny gender thing: Male chefs often don't like sharing their best recipes, but the women always seem willing to write them down or talk them through, passing on the tips they discovered as they perfected the dishes.

Miriam brought this recipe to the catering company back in the '80s, and it's been on the menu ever since. It uses a dark and delicious marinade that I crave. I like to serve the chicken in large pieces, either halves or quarter birds. It's best eaten with the hands. Make sure your guests love birds on bones—not everybody does.

Prep time: 15 minutes
Cooking time: 45 minutes
Serves 4

1/2 cup honey
1/2 cup soy sauce or tamari
1/2 cup red wine
1 tablespoon fresh lemon juice
1/4 cup shredded basil leaves (about 5 stalks)
1 chicken, halved or quartered

Whisk together honey, soy sauce, wine, and lemon juice in a large bowl until well combined. Add basil. Add chicken to the bowl and turn to coat with marinade, or place chicken in large plastic bag, pour in marinade, and seal tightly. Cover and marinate 24 hours in the refrigerator.

Preheat oven to 425°. Remove chicken from marinade and place skin-side up in a roasting pan. Roast for 15 minutes; the skin should be blistering. Reduce heat to 375 and roast another 30 minutes. Check doneness with an internal thermometer—I recommend 160 degrees.

SWEET BARBECUED BRISKET

I didn't know what brisket was until Chelsea, my manager for a while, told me I should add her Nanni's brisket to our catering menu. We never had it growing up Pennsylvania Dutch; slow-roasted meats were limited to pot roast. Chelsea was right about the brisket—to this day, it remains one of our most popular entrées. During our restaurant years, we made it every single day to keep up with demand. Chelsea and I parted ways many years ago, shortly after I opened the restaurant, but I'll always have a soft spot in my heart for her Nanni's brisket.

A delicious brisket takes a good long while in a slow oven. If you're using a grass-fed cut, roast it a little longer, up to an additional hour, until it's fork-tender.

Prep time: 15 minutes
Cooking time: 3 1/2 hours
Serves 8 to 10

2 tablespoons paprika	3/4 cup brown sugar
1 tablespoon granulated garlic	1 cup ketchup
1 tablespoon sugar	1 cup tomato sauce
1 tablespoon sea salt	1/4 cup horseradish
1 tablespoon fresh pepper	2 tablespoons Worcestershire or soy sauce
1 brisket, trimmed, about 5 pounds	2 cups water

Preheat oven to 400°. In a small bowl, stir together paprika, granulated garlic, sugar, salt, and pepper and rub all over meat. Place brisket in a roasting pan, fat side up, and roast, uncovered, until brown, about 50 minutes.

While brisket is roasting, make sauce. Place brown sugar, ketchup, tomato sauce, horseradish, Worcestershire, and water in medium bowl and whisk until sugar is dissolved. Set aside.

After 50 minutes, reduce oven to 325°. Remove brisket from oven and pour sauce over the meat. Cover tightly with a lid or foil and roast for 2 1/2 hours. Remove meat from sauce and allow meat to cool, overnight if possible, saving the sauce separately. To serve, slice brisket against the grain and reheat gently in the sauce, adding a splash of water if the sauce is too thick.

Potatoes Anna for a crowd

My girlfriend Michelle loves potatoes. She really, really loves them. Whenever we get together for family dinners or potlucks, we know her offering will somehow involve Yukon golds or russets. One time for her birthday we did an entire meal of potato dishes. I'm not kidding, and as dopey as it sounds, it was an amazing potatolicious celebration. To add to the gaiety, our friend Shelley brought party favors of little sweet potato growing kits, and you know what? I planted that little sprouted potato and got twelve more sweet potatoes. Do you see why I love these ladies?

Typically, Potatoes Anna is a pretty little potato tart crisped on the stovetop and finished in the oven. This version is done completely in the oven. It's simple and satisfying; the crunchy potato crust is the best part.

Prep time: 15 minutes
Cooking time: 1 hour to 1 hour and 15 minutes
Serves 8 to 12

1/2 cup to 1 cup olive oil, divided
1/2 cup water
5 cloves garlic, minced
1 tablespoon sea salt, plus more to finish
2 teaspoons freshly ground pepper
2 tablespoons (1/2 bunch) parsley leaves, minced
4 to 5 pounds red or yellow potatoes,
        sliced thin by hand or with a mandoline

Preheat oven to 400°. Grease a large roasting pan or cast iron skillet with a tablespoon of olive oil. In a large bowl, stir together 3/4 cup olive oil, water, garlic, most of the parsley (save a little), salt, and pepper. Add potatoes and toss until evenly coated. Layer potatoes thoughtfully in the bottom of the pan, repeating the process until you've used all the potatoes. Scrape any extra liquid from the bowl over potatoes and press them down real snug with your hands or the back of a spatula. Cover tightly with a lid or foil and roast for 30 minutes.

Reduce heat to 350°. Remove foil and press the potatoes again with the back of a spatula and drizzle with additional olive oil if they look dry. Roast an additional 30 minutes. Test for doneness by inserting a knife in the middle of the pan—it should slide in and out easily. If it's not done, keep cooking and test every 10 minutes. Sprinkle with extra parsley, salt (try a designer salt if you have some), and up to a 1/4 cup olive oil. Serve in the pan.

INDRA'S JAFFNA POTATOES

In 1987, I met an amazing woman who became my lifelong friend. She was having some issues with her man, so she brought her two young sons (four and five years old) to Los Angeles to try something new. This wouldn't seem exceptional except for the fact that she had moved from Sri Lanka. Over the course of the next twenty years, Indra helped me raise my kids, baked my desserts, opened a daycare, and became a citizen. She gave my son a true appreciation of spicy chiles, and she taught me how to make these aromatic potatoes. It's pretty much the recipe that serves as the base for any kind of curry. She likes to make it with chicken thighs or shrimp instead of the potatoes, and it's also delicious with green vegetables or cauliflower. I love to make this, mostly because I love Indra.

Prep time: 20 minutes
Cooking time: About 1 hour
Serves 8 to 10

1 tablespoon mustard seed
3 cardamom pods or
   1/2 teaspoon ground
2 bay leaves
2 cinnamon sticks, about 3 inches long
3 tablespoons olive oil
4 cloves garlic, minced
2 tablespoons minced ginger

1 small red onion, diced (about 1 cup)
1 teaspoon to 1 tablespoon diced
   jalapeño, to taste
2 pounds Yukon gold or other waxy-skin
   potatoes, chopped into a large dice
2 cups fresh or canned diced tomatoes
1 teaspoon sea salt
2 teaspoons cider vinegar

In a large, dry skillet on high heat, toast mustard seed, cardamom, bay leaves, and cinnamon sticks until mustard seeds pop. Add oil, garlic, ginger, onion, and 1 teaspoon jalapeño and sauté everything together until lightly browned, about 4 minutes. Add potatoes and stir to coat with the spice mixture. Cook until potatoes are lightly browned, about 10 minutes. Add diced tomatoes, reduce heat to a simmer, and cover. Cook until potatoes are soft, another 35 minutes or so. Add salt, vinegar, and more jalapeño according to your preference for heat. Remove the pods, bay leaves, and cinnamon sticks before serving.

ROASTED POTATO SALAD

My best friend growing up was Jo. She was also my second cousin and, for a few wonderful years, my neighbor. Her mom, Floss (Chef Ma's cousin, although I remain baffled as to the connection), taught us how to play pinochle after school and helped us get every Girl Scout badge we ever wanted and then some. I saw her Great Dane give birth to six puppies (yes, I was scarred for life), and I fell in love with Floss's Apple Brown Betty. (We call it Fruit Crumble, and you'll find it on page 87.)

Jo loved potatoes. I would say she lurved them. One time, I watched her open a can, take out a perfect white globe and eat it. She told me it was a potato, but I had never seen one like THAT before. This potato salad is for you, Jo—we may be separated by most of a continent, but I know you're still catching my light, and I am still catching yours.

Be sure not to roast these potatoes too much. They need to be soft all the way through but not dark brown, because then the centers will dry out. Serve warm for best results.

Prep time: 15 minutes
Cooking time: 20 to 30 minutes
Serves 4 to 6

2 pounds red or yellow potatoes, skins on, cut into a large dice
2 tablespoons olive oil
3/4 teaspoon sea salt
1/2 teaspoon freshly ground pepper
1/2 cup mayonnaise
2 tablespoons grainy mustard
4 green onions, cut into 1/4-inch rounds

Preheat oven to 375°. In a large bowl, toss potatoes, olive oil, salt, and pepper together until well coated. Spread on a rimmed baking sheet and roast until cooked through and lightly browned, 20 to 30 minutes. After 15 minutes, carefully flip the potatoes with a spatula without tearing them. Check for doneness and set aside to cool.

In the same large bowl, whisk together mayonnaise and mustard. Add cooled potatoes and green onions. Toss all to coat. Serve immediately.

Melissa's Peanut Butter Blondies
with Chocolate Ganache

I had an amazing manager at the Double Dutch restaurant, Miss Melissa the sugar-plum vegan. She was a powerhouse in hospitality and human resources and a phenomenal vegan baker. She sold her vegan muffins at farmers' markets during the day and ran the restaurant at night, acting as sommelier, general manager, and expediter. Now she's raising her beautiful family in Sacramento and thriving at her very own Sugar Plum Vegan Bakery. This recipe is for you, sweet Melissa—thank you for all you taught me about plant-based goodness, coconut milk, and flax.

Prep time: 30 minutes
Cooking time: 40 minutes
Makes 12 large or 24 small blondies

1 1/2 cups peanut butter
   (crunchy or smooth)
2/3 cup neutral-tasting oil
1 1/2 tablespoons vanilla extract
2 cups brown sugar
1 teaspoon ground ginger
2 cups flour
1 teaspoon sea salt
1 teaspoon baking powder
1/2 cup milk (soy, rice, or almond)
2/3 cup whole unsalted peanuts

1 14-ounce can coconut milk
1 coconut-milk can's worth (about 1 1/2
   cups) of semi-sweet chocolate chips

Preheat oven to 325°. In the bowl of an electric mixer, add peanut butter, oil, vanilla, brown sugar, and ginger. Mix at a low speed until blended. Add flour, salt, baking powder, milk, and peanuts and mix at a low speed until well blended. Spread mixture into an ungreased 9" x 13" baking dish. Bake for 20 minutes. Rotate the pan and bake until the blondies start pulling away from the sides of the pan, about 20 more minutes.

While blondies cool, make the ganache. In a small saucepan, heat coconut milk over medium-low heat until warm. Fill the coconut milk can with chocolate chips and add them to the saucepan. Give it a stir, turn off the heat, and let sit on the burner with the heat off until the chips are melted and the mixture can be stirred like an icing. (Taste testing with your fingers is absolutely necessary for this recipe to be successful. Chef's orders.)

Spread ganache on top of the lightly cooled blondies. Refrigerate for 2 hours or overnight before cutting and serving.

Cooking on Vacation

Every August I go to my happy place with my family and friends for two weeks of oceanfront bliss on the central coast of California. We rent a house and like to have our meals together, but a table of fourteen every night can be a total buzzkill on holiday, even for a pro like me. So a few years back, I created a little chart of all fourteen days and assigned everyone (teenagers and older) three entrées and six sides that they're responsible for sometime in the two weeks. Once again, I had free time at the beach. We keep it super simple—lots of local produce, a night or two out, and tacos from a local stand for lunch. And maybe every single night we have homemade gelato from the candy store in town.

When it comes to packing, I make sure I have my essentials: my favorite knives, a mandoline, a flexible spatula, and a couple of spring-loaded tongs. We tend to be beverage guzzlers, so I also pack a box of quart-size Ball jars for beach beverages and leftovers. I bring a pile of my tea towels, coffee beans, and our grinder. I freeze a cooked brisket, I get some fatty roasters from the chicken man (and hide the $25 price tag from Chef Ma), and I bring a lamb leg and some pork ribs.

Please oh please, keep it simple! One year, newlyweds Finn and Dawn opted for a pizza night with a big Caesar salad—we loved it! And my holiday wouldn't be complete without my friend Kathleen's schnitzel. Pounded thin and served with lemon wedges, it is a fried delight the kids go crazy for. The nice part is while she's pounding away, others are making the salad and sides. Many hands make light work and a better vacation.

I have to share the oddest thing I take on holiday: twelve pounds of Taylor Pork Roll, which we grew up eating in Pennsylvania. It's a bizarre cured-pork product packed into a canvas bag. You slice it up, fry it in butter, and eat it on a soft white roll with mustard. It's not as weird as scrapple, but still, it's odd. My sister calls it a flat hot dog, and it's our thing.

My best advice for vacation eating? Do your thing. Just keep it simple.

Chapter Five

Slowing Down in Spain

we went on holiday

I was fortunate enough to experience my first European holiday in the summer of 2004. We spent two weeks at the Casa de Ferrando in the Catalonia region of northern Spain with friends and family. Total head count: eight kids + six adults = fourteen of us.

It took me a few days to adjust, as I found the jet lag to be worse than I expected, and I was anxious to go, see, do—it took me forever to get to Europe, and I wanted to get busy!

Thankfully, slowing down came easy.

Our spacious villa in the sleepy village of Fornells de la Selva, an hour north of Barcelona, was an oasis with plenty of room and our own pool. We were in the countryside in the middle of a nursery. We quickly settled into our holiday home, creating a sprawling dinner table on the back veranda where we could all gather. We found the local bakery, the *carnisseria*, the only restaurant in town, and the grocery.

With the size of our posse, food was a constant topic, and we quickly befriended the butcher and the baker. I started to relax and stop running on overdrive. I fell in love with Spain again every single day. The pace of the day was like nothing I'd ever experienced. Breakfast was a lazy gathering around fresh croissants, crusty breads, dried meats, and Manchego cheese. There were local tomatoes, peaches, and cherries and strong, dark coffee. We put a big jar of Nutella on the table, and there was always the local aioli.

We usually had lunch while we were out wandering around the country. The *menú del dia*, a four-course lunch offered by every restaurant, was by far the best deal, averaging nine euros a person. We drank the wine dispensed from beer taps and always started with the house gazpacho, followed by an appetizer, the main course, and dessert. Naturally, after such a generous lunch, the entire population is forced to go home and take a nap—genius!

Every business shut down from three to six. There was no shopping after lunch, and since we'd scheduled naps, why not have the wine? Dinner was never earlier than nine. We easily adjusted to this European lifestyle and spent many an evening on the back veranda, feasting on *plats cuinats* (prepared dishes) from our friends at Can Tonet, the *carnisseria*, or the local restaurant.

We all became addicted to the suave Spanish gazpacho. I grew up with chunky, red Mexican-style gazpacho, but I'll never go back to that. The gazpacho recipe in this chapter is heaven during tomato season—try it and you'll see what I mean.

traditional SPANISH GAZPACHO

This is a fantastic cold soup, smooth and creamy despite the lack of dairy. The authentic recipe results in gazpacho with a beautiful peach tone, unlike any version I've had stateside. The secret, I learned in Catalonia, is adding a chunk of stale bread and a drizzle of strong, green extra-virgin olive oil. The lush finish comes from sieving the soup before chilling. As with the Spanish tortilla, measurements are usually at the whim of the chef, so feel free to experiment a little. I hear the locals keep this soup in their refrigerators like we keep iced tea.

Prep time: About 20 minutes, plus several hours of chilling time
Serves 6

2 pounds (about 1 quart) ripe tomatoes, quartered
1 small cucumber, peeled and roughly chopped
1 small red bell pepper, seeded and roughly chopped
1 chunk stale white bread, about the size of an egg,
    softened with water
1 teaspoon sea salt
1/2 teaspoon white pepper
1/4 teaspoon ground cumin
1 tablespoon wine vinegar (either kind)
4 tablespoons extra-virgin olive oil

Place tomatoes, cucumber, bell pepper, bread, salt, pepper, cumin, and vinegar in a blender with a tight-fitting lid and purée. With the motor running, slowly drizzle in the olive oil and blend thoroughly. Strain through a fine sieve. Discard solids and taste, adjusting salt and pepper to taste. Chill several hours before serving, preferably overnight. Serve very cold.

CLASSIC POTATO CROQUETAS

Oh croqueta, you are a deep-fried wonder. Each little gem is just like a tater tot, only better because it's homemade. It shouldn't be bigger than two bites, and preferably it can be popped in your mouth in its entirety. If you like little fried things as much as I do, try frying green olives, amazingly perfect served alongside these croquetas. Also, find a recipe for date and blue cheese croquetas. Talk about authentic. Basically you beat a thick béchamel into submission until almost dry with the melted dates and blue cheese. It's then chilled and develops the same powerhouse of flavor that is the potato croqueta, only with the intensity of blue cheese and medjool dates. The date croqueta recipe is a tad scary to tackle, but I support anyone facing their fears in the kitchen. Do it!

This potato croqueta recipe, on the other hand, is a straightforward and easy crowd pleaser, equally suited to cocktail-hour tapas or a fun dish on a family-style dinner table. Serve them with aioli, and you can make them a little bit ahead—they taste as good at room temperature as piping hot. You can use half Yukon gold potatoes if you like, but they have more gluten than russets, so let them fall apart while simmering to release the starch.

Prep time: 30 to 45 minutes
Cooking time: 15 minutes for potatoes plus 12 to 18 minutes for croquetas
Makes about 24 croquetas

6 medium russet potatoes (2 1/2 pounds), peeled and quartered
1 teaspoon granulated onion
1 teaspoon granulated garlic
1/2 teaspoon sea salt
1/4 cup grated parmesan
1 tablespoon chopped fresh parsley or 1 teaspoon dried
1/2 teaspoon white pepper
3 large eggs, divided
1/2 pound firm mozzarella, chopped or grated
1 cup fine dry breadcrumbs (*see recipe page 37*)
About 2 1/2 cups olive oil

In a large pot, cover potatoes with salted cold water, bring to a boil, reduce heat, and simmer until tender, about 15 minutes. Drain potatoes and cool slightly.

Mash potatoes with granulated onion and garlic, salt, parmesan, parsley, and pepper. Stir in 1 egg, then fold in mozzarella.

Form potato mixture into 24 oblong croquettes (about a scant 1/4 cup each). Lightly beat remaining 2 eggs in a shallow bowl and put breadcrumbs in another shallow bowl. Dip 1 croqueta into eggs, letting excess drip off, then roll in breadcrumbs to coat. Transfer to a baking sheet. Repeat with remaining croquetas.

Heat 1/2 inch oil (about 2 1/2 cups) in a 12-inch heavy skillet over medium-high heat. Before it starts smoking (olive oil can burn), fry croquetas in batches until golden brown, about 3 minutes per side. Serve with aoili (see below).

SUPER EASY AIOLI

Makes about 1 cup

3/4 cup mayonnaise (*see recipe page 27*)
Juice of 1/2 lemon (about 1 tablespoon)
1 tablespoon parsley, minced
1/4 teaspoon freshly ground pepper
2 garlic cloves, minced

Combine all ingredients in a medium bowl and whisk together. Cover and chill until ready to serve. For a classic red pepper aioli, substitute minced roasted red pepper for the parsley.

Basque Red Pepper Chicken

This is a delicious savory chicken that really celebrates the bell pepper. A fan of all things sweet, I use the yellow and red, but if you like sharper green bell peppers, go for it. It works best with chicken on the bone. Cut the peppers into tidy, equal-size squares or julienne them—it'll taste better.

Prep time: 30 minutes
Cooking time: 50 minutes
Serves 4 to 8, depending on how many other dishes you serve

2 tablespoons olive oil
4 chicken drumsticks
4 chicken thighs
1 teaspoon sea salt
1/2 teaspoon freshly ground pepper
1 large onion, diced
1 red bell pepper, seeded and chopped
1/2 yellow bell pepper, seeded and chopped
3 cloves garlic, minced
2 teaspoons paprika
20 cherry tomatoes cut in half, or 2 cups chopped fresh roma tomatoes
2 sprigs fresh thyme or 1/2 teaspoon dried thyme
1 cup dry white wine
1/4 cup brandy
1/2 cup stock (any kind) or water
2 ounces Serrano ham, diced

Preheat oven to 400°. In a large, deep ovenproof skillet, heat the oil. Season the chicken with salt and pepper and add to the skillet, skin side down. Cook over moderately high heat until browned, about 4 minutes per side. Transfer the chicken to a large plate, skin side up.

Add onion, peppers, garlic, and paprika to the skillet and cook over medium heat, stirring occasionally until softened, about 10 minutes. Add cherry tomatoes and thyme; once the tomatoes are hot, pour in the wine and brandy and simmer over high heat for 1 minute. Stir in the stock or water and bring to a boil. Return the chicken to the skillet, skin side up. Cover tightly and braise in the oven for about 10 minutes. Remove the lid and cook until the chicken is cooked through, about 10 more minutes.

Transfer the chicken to a large serving dish. With a slotted spoon, transfer the vegetables to the serving dish. Boil the remaining cooking liquid over high heat until reduced to 1 cup, about 10 minutes. Add Serrano ham and bring to a simmer. Remove from heat and taste to see if the sauce needs salt or pepper. Pour over the chicken and vegetables and serve.

ARROZ CON POLLO Y PAELLA

For one special dinner on our terrace in Fornells, our local butcher at Can Tonet made us beautiful paella. We borrowed his 24-inch paella pan and returned it empty the next morning when we stopped in for our croissants and baguettes. See how easy it is to love Spain?

It's important to use a quality rice. I'm quite fond of risotto rice, in particular the arborio and carnaroli. But if you have access to a nice Spanish rice, try that! You can make it with brown rice, but you'll need to add an extra cup of liquid. I like short-grain brown rice best, but I know others who prefer long-grain—it's at the whim of the chef.

This is a recipe for arroz con pollo, but you can easily transform it into paella by adding a dozen pieces of shellfish during the last ten minutes of cooking and subbing Spanish chorizo for the hot Italian sausage.

This can also be a great vegan entrée: Just leave out the animal products and add sautéed artichoke hearts and legumes.

Prep time: 30 minutes
Cooking time: 50 minutes
Serves 10

1 pound hot Italian sausage (whole links)
1 pound boneless chicken thighs (skin on or off as you prefer),
    lightly seasoned with salt and pepper
2 tablespoons extra-virgin olive oil
1 white onion, diced
6 garlic cloves, minced
1 red bell pepper, seeded and diced
1 teaspoon dried oregano
1 tablespoon smoked paprika
1 3/4 cups short-grain Spanish rice or arborio rice
1 1/2 cups fresh or canned diced tomatoes, with juice
Generous pinch saffron threads
6 cups chicken or vegetable stock, plus more if needed
1 cup green beans, trimmed and cut into 1-1/2-inch pieces
1 bunch parsley, leaves only, chopped

Preheat oven to 375°. In your largest ovenproof skillet or paella pan, sear sausage over medium heat until almost cooked through, about 10 minutes. Remove links from the pan and set aside. Brown chicken thighs in the same pan, taking particular care to sear the skin if it's attached. Remove chicken from the pan and slice both the sausage and chicken thighs into two or three chunks each. Set aside.

In the same skillet, add olive oil and sauté onion, garlic, red pepper, oregano, and paprika until lightly browned over medium-high heat. Add the rice and stir for 2 minutes before adding tomatoes, saffron, and 4 cups of stock. Scrape up any brown bits on the bottom of the skillet. Stir, add chicken and sausage, and bring to a simmer over medium heat. Add green beans. Pour 2 cups of stock over the top and seal with a tight-fitting lid or foil. Roast in the oven for 20 minutes. Check to see if the rice is tender, adding more stock if needed. Sprinkle with minced parsley, let rest for 15 minutes, and serve directly from the skillet or paella pan.

TORTILLA DE PATATAS

I don't think I had a single tortilla when we were in Spain. I'm not even sure I knew what it was when I was there. (In Spain, tortillas are a crustless potato and egg pie.) What I can tell you is this: My daughter spent a summer in Spain during her college days and upon her return made us the best *tortilla de patatas* ever. She makes small six-inch tortillas using the method below.

Salting your eggs before adding them to the batter is important—a key component in giving flavor to the finished product. And you're going to need a large plate or tray to invert the tortilla onto, so choose your frying pan appropriately.

On the advice of Ferran Adrià, I've made this with Cape Cod Kettle Chips instead of fresh potatoes, and I have to say...delicious.

While this is the traditional recipe, a tortilla's possibilities are endless. Try it with any vegetable (go green with kale or spinach), cooked or uncooked, and call it a frittata!

Prep time: 15 minutes
Cooking time: 25 minutes for potatoes, 15 minutes for tortilla
Serves 6 to 8 for tapas or 4 as a main dish

2 1/2 to 3 pounds Yukon gold potatoes, peeled and thinly sliced
1 1/2 teaspoons sea salt, divided
1/4 cup plus 2 tablespoons olive oil, divided
1 small onion, quartered and thinly sliced (about 1 cup)
5 large eggs
2 tablespoons water
Chopped parsley, if desired

In a large bowl, toss potatoes with 1 teaspoon salt. Heat 1/4 cup olive oil in a heavy 9-inch skillet over medium-high heat until very hot, about 3 minutes. Add all the potatoes and cook, stirring often to prevent the potatoes from sticking and browning, until they are partially cooked, about 7 minutes. Stir in onion, reduce heat to medium, and continue cooking until potatoes are completely soft, about 15 more minutes. Return to the bowl and let them cool for about 10 minutes.

In a smaller bowl, beat eggs, water, and 1/2 teaspoon salt until just combined. Add to cooled potato mixture and flip potatoes with a fork to get them all soaked in the egg batter, breaking them up for maximum submersion. Let rest for 10 minutes.

Using the same skillet, heat 2 tablespoons olive oil until almost smoking, about 4 minutes. Pour the egg-potato mixture into the skillet and reduce the heat to medium-low. Cook, moving and shaking the skillet, running a thin metal spatula around the edge and sliding it into the middle so that some of the egg from the center runs under the edges, like you would with an omelet. Cook until the top is no longer liquid, 6 to 8 minutes. Run the spatula completely under the tortilla to make sure that no part of the bottom is stuck to the skillet.

Now you need to flip over the tortilla. Top the skillet with a rimless plate slightly larger than the skillet and, using oven mitts, quickly invert the tortilla onto the plate and return the skillet to the stove. If the skillet looks dry, add a little more olive oil. Carefully slide the tortilla back into the skillet, uncooked side down. Shake the skillet to straighten the tortilla and push the edges in with the spatula. Reduce the heat to very low and cook until a toothpick inserted in the center comes out clean, 3 to 5 more minutes. Alternatively, instead of flipping the tortilla, you can broil it under a preheated broiler for 6 to 8 minutes.

Invert the tortilla onto a serving plate. Let it cool for a few minutes, sprinkling with chopped parsley if desired. Cut into wedges and serve warm or at room temperature.

RUSTIC FRUIT TART

When Chef Ma was little, her family had their own version of this Rustic Tart: slop pie. I know, it's a terrible name. But it wasn't a terrible pie. Slop pie is a cute mini pie made from leftover pie crusts and fillings. If there was no filling left over, a dab of butter, cinnamon, and sugar would do the trick. The point is not to fuss. It's supposed to be uneven and a little broken. I really like to pour on the sugar before I put it in the oven—it's like fairy dust that bakes into the fruit so nicely.

This rustic tart works with any fruit, but it's especially delicious with blood oranges, like I have below, or with peaches and a mix of berries. And if you don't feel like making the pie crust and pull one out of the freezer instead, that's fine by me!

Prep time: 30 minutes plus chilling time
Cooking time: 60 to 75 minutes
Serves 4 to 6

1 pie crust (*see recipe page 186, or a storebought one is fine*)
3 blood oranges or 1 cup of your fruit of choice
4 ounces cream cheese, room temperature
4 or more tablespoons sugar, divided
1 tablespoon vanilla extract
Zest of 1 orange
1 egg yolk mixed with 2 tablespoons water

Preheat oven to 350°. Line a rimmed baking sheet with parchment paper and lay out the pie crust. Roll dough flat into a 14-inch circle; don't worry if the edges are rough.

Slice off the peel on either end of the oranges. Stand them on end, peel them with a knife, then turn them on their sides and cut into 1/2-inch-thick rounds, removing any seeds. Set aside on a plate. In a small bowl, mix cream cheese with 3 tablespoons sugar, vanilla, and orange zest. Blend well and spread in the middle of the pie shell to cover about 6 inches in the center. Arrange oranges on top of the cream cheese, leaving a 2-inch border of dough all around. Sprinkle with 3 tablespoons sugar. Fold dough partially over fruit, leaving most of the fruit in the center uncovered. Brush dough with egg wash and sprinkle again with 1 tablespoon sugar (at least).

Position a rack in the center of the oven. Bake the tart until the fruit is bubbling and the pastry is golden brown, 60 to 75 minutes, depending on the thickness of the crust. Allow to cool completely before serving.

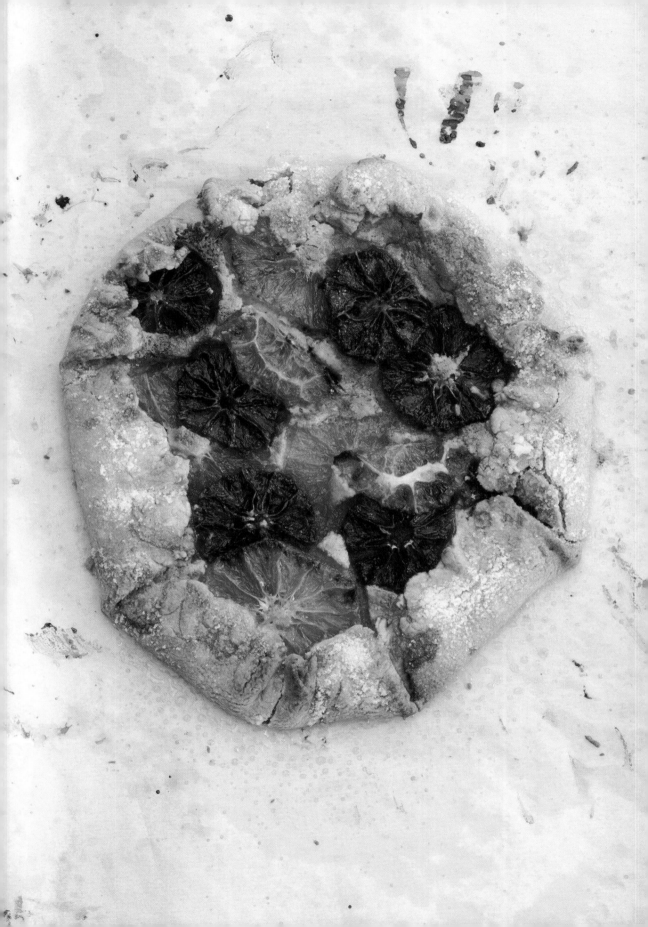

7 Tasty Flavor Profiles

Mix and match for a delicious dinner

SWEET – fruits and grains
SOUR – fermented foods, vinegar
SALTY – natural salt
BITTER – dark leafy greens, herbs, and spices
UMAMI – mushroomy, soy sauce or tamari, asparagus, meaty
PUNGENT – chiles, garlic, herbs, and spices
ASTRINGENT – legumes and vegetables

Chapter SIX
Sustainable Suppers

Plant Based Parties

When I got back from Spain, everything changed. I was renewed from being far away, rested and ready to try new things. For starters, I realized I could slow down and support my community more, like I did on holiday. I was more committed to using local offerings from farmers' markets. Which was easy, because we had a sweet and petite market around the corner from the restaurant in the heart of Culver City.

Inspired by and envious of the secret supper club buzz in San Francisco, I wanted to be the first in town to do the same, so I started the Sustainable Supper Club, a monthly vegan dinner party featuring local offerings. I'd pick a theme and create a five-course, family-style, plant-based feast ending with a delicious dessert. Menu planning was tricky. There's no main course necessary in a plant-based menu—everything is a main dish, everything is a side dish, and all are interchangeable. The goal is to mix textures, colors, and flavors and let the powerful simplicity of the vegetables be the star.

Then and now, I balance out the menu with potatoes, pasta, or rice, and I make sure to have five servings of vegetables at every meal. In my book, that is a successful plant-based party menu.

Our favorite way to serve supper at the catering company is family style. We aren't real good at fussy, plated, white-glove service—we like to share. It's important that the serving plates aren't hot, so they can be passed, and they shouldn't be too large. We use 10-inch dinner plates as serving platters and little tongs. Serve soupy sauces separately to minimize spillage; a little bowl and an espresso spoon are perfect for this.

If cooking an entire meal by yourself makes you shake in your boots, ask your friends to bring something, but don't call it a potluck. Be specific. If you're making the lasagna, someone can bring a salad or green beans and someone else can bring dessert and a loaf of bread. Share the load, it's more relaxing. It also makes your friends feel good to participate.

Be sure to have the appetizers set up before you put on your party garb, and have the bar area arranged with ice, glassware, and libations both alcoholic and nonalcoholic. Once all the elements are lined up for a great party, it's time to let it flow and enjoy yourself.

Quinoa Fritters

Quinoa is one of those ancient "new" foods that can take some getting used to. Thankfully, this recipe will make a lover out of any doubters. When it's fried up, the quinoa gets a crispy crust that's very satisfying. It's a nice addition to any table and a great dish to share. People love fritters. Make them half the size for a tasty appetizer.

Prep time: 20 to 25 minutes
Cooking time: 20 to 24 minutes, plus quinoa cooking time
Makes 12 fritters

2 tablespoons olive oil, plus 1/2 cup
  for frying
1/2 cup minced onion
1/4 cup minced carrot
1/4 cup minced celery
1/4 cup minced red pepper
3 garlic cloves, minced

1 cup cooked quinoa
1/2 cup breadcrumbs (*see recipe page 37*)
1/4 cup whole-wheat flour
1 teaspoon sea salt
1/2 teaspoon freshly ground pepper
1 tablespoon minced parsley or cilantro

Heat a large sauté pan over medium heat. Add 2 tablespoons oil and sauté onion, carrot, celery, pepper, and garlic until translucent, about 7 minutes. Transfer to a large bowl and add cooked quinoa, breadcrumbs, flour, salt, pepper, and parsley or cilantro. Mix well. Squeezing the batter together firmly, form mixture into 12 3-inch fritters (24 if you want mini-fritters). Add 1/2 cup olive oil to sauté pan and heat over medium-high heat until hot but not smoking. Fry the fritters in small batches until golden brown, less than 2 minutes per side. Serve with Creamy Mushroom Gravy (see next page).

Creamy Mushroom Gravy

This versatile vegan gravy works with almost any savory dish. One of my secret ingredients for delicious vegan sauces is vegan cream cheese substitute, which you can find at your more evolved markets and health food stores. I use it to replace heavy cream, cream cheese, chèvre, and tofu. It has a creamier consistency than tofu, and it thins really well with a little coconut or rice milk.

Prep time: 10 minutes
Cooking time: 10 to 15 minutes
Makes about 1 1/2 cups

2 tablespoons olive oil
2 garlic cloves, minced
1 shallot, minced, or 1/4 cup minced onion
2 cups sliced mushrooms, any type or combination
1 bay leaf
1 sprig fresh thyme or 1/4 teaspoon dried thyme
1/2 cup white wine or Marsala
4 ounces vegan cream cheese (1/2 tub), or heavy cream if you're not cooking vegan
1 tablespoon light-colored miso
3/4 cup additional liquid to thin: milk (rice, almond, or soy), stock, or water

In a large skillet over medium-high heat, heat oil and sauté garlic, shallots, mushrooms, bay leaf, and thyme. When shallots start to brown after about 6 minutes, deglaze the pan by adding white wine or Marsala. With the heat on medium, reduce the liquid by half, about 6 minutes. Add vegan cream cheese, whisking and smashing the cheese until melted and smooth. Remove bay leaf and thyme twigs and whisk in additional liquid until gravy thins to desired consistency.

Sweet Potato Fritters

Sweet potatoes are finally getting their well-deserved spotlight. These fritters are one of our most popular dishes at the catering company, and not just for vegans. The sweet potato caramelizes and adds great flavor.

Prep time: 30 minutes
Cooking time: 20 minutes, plus 1 hour to cook sweet potatoes
Makes 12 large or 16 small fritters

3 tablespoons olive oil, plus more if needed
1/2 cup minced red pepper
1/2 teaspoon chopped fresh thyme
1 1/2 pounds sweet potatoes, roasted until soft and peeled
3/4 cup breadcrumbs (*see recipe page 37*), divided
3/4 cup coarsely ground pistachios, divided
1 teaspoon cinnamon
1 tablespoon maple syrup
1/2 teaspoon sea salt
1/4 teaspoon freshly ground pepper

HOW TO ROAST A SWEET POTATO

Preheat oven to 350°. Wash and remove intense blemishes from potatoes and place on a baking sheet or directly on the rack. Roast until tender, about 1 hour, checking at 45 minutes.

Heat 2 teaspoons oil over medium-high heat and sauté red pepper and thyme until soft, about 5 minutes. Transfer to a large bowl and add sweet potatoes, 1/2 cup breadcrumbs, 1/2 cup pistachios, cinnamon, maple syrup, salt, and pepper. Mix until well combined and shape into 3-inch patty-style fritters (or smaller if you like). In a pie plate, combine remaining 1/4 cup breadcrumbs and 1/4 cup pistachios. Press fritters into breadcrumb-nut mixture on both sides. Heat 2 tablespoons oil in a large skillet over medium heat. Fry patties in small batches (no touching!) until brown, about 3 minutes on each side, using more oil as needed. Serve with Cilantro Crema and Boozy Blackberry Balsamic Reduction (*see next page*).

VARIATION:
For a gluten-free alternative, replace the breadcrumbs with macerated crispy rice cereal or coarsely ground quick oats.

WHO WANTS SECONDS?

Boozy Blackberry Balsamic REDUCTION

This makes everything double yum. We keep it in a squeeze bottle at the Shoppe and use it daily. It adds pow to everything it touches and makes simple vegetables extra appealing.

Prep time: 10 minutes
Cooking time: 25 minutes
Makes about 2 cups

1 1/2 cups blackberries
2 cups balsamic vinegar
1 cup Port or Cabernet
1 cup sugar

Rinse blackberries and combine with vinegar, wine, and sugar in a saucepan, stainless steel preferred. Cook over medium heat until reduced by half, about 20 minutes, smashing the blackberries while cooking to make the most of their flavor. Remove from heat and strain the sauce through a sieve to remove the seeds. Return to the pan and cook an additional 5 minutes or so, until it has the consistency of maple syrup. The reduction will thicken as it cools, so be careful not to overcook. The sauce can be thinned with more vinegar or water should it get too thick. Store in a squeeze bottle or clean jar; it will keep in the refrigerator for months.

Cilantro Crema

Crema is our version of vegan sour cream. Here, it's blended with cilantro; you can use all sorts of herbs. If you want to serve some plain crema alongside the flavored one, remove half before adding the cilantro, and use half the cilantro.

Prep time: 10 minutes
Makes 1 1/3 cups

8 ounces vegan cream cheese
1 teaspoon fresh lemon juice
1/4 cup rice milk
1/2 bunch cilantro, minced

Place cream cheese, lemon juice, and 2 tablespoons rice milk in blender and blend until combined. Add the remaining milk 1 tablespoon at a time until you achieve a sour cream–like consistency. Pulse in cilantro. Do not over-process unless you want a green crema. Chill and drizzle in more rice milk to thin as needed before serving. Serve with fritters, raw vegetables, or any dish suitable for dipping.

Mix 'n' match: Here we paired up Massaged Kale & Quinoa
with the Honey Roasted Carrots on page 79.

Massaged Kale & Quinoa

I know, it seems crazy to give a salad a massage to make it wilt, but I'm a believer, especially with kale. The trick is to get in there with your clean hands and make that chemical change happen, so the kale softens. I've massaged with just salt as well, but the results are superior when using a dressing as the catalyst. And when you use your hands to spread the love, there's an extra bonus in it for the diners.

Prep time: 25 minutes, including cooking quinoa
Serves 6

DRESSING

3 tablespoons extra-virgin olive oil
1/4 cup cider vinegar
1 tablespoon maple syrup
1 teaspoon fresh lemon juice
1 teaspoon chile powder

1 teaspoon prepared mustard, any kind
1/2 teaspoon smoked paprika
1/2 teaspoon sea salt
1/4 teaspoon freshly ground pepper

SALAD

1 bunch kale (about 1 pound), any variety, stems removed and leaves shredded
1/2 cup quinoa, cooked according to package directions and cooled
    (about 1 1/2 cups cooked)
1 orange, peeled and cut into sections
1 cup cherry tomatoes, cut in half
1/2 cup diced red onion
1/2 cup toasted sunflower seeds

In a small bowl, whisk all the dressing ingredients together, or put them in a jar with a tight-fitting lid, seal, and shake.

Place kale in a large bowl, pour the dressing over it, and massage with your hands until the kale gets softer, shinier, and less bulky, about 2 minutes. Add quinoa, oranges, cherry tomatoes, red onion, and sunflower seeds. Toss well and chill until serving time. This salad gets more delicious as it ages—it'll keep a few days.

FENNEL SLAW

Fennel is another crazy vegetable. There are times at the local farmers' markets when it is so huge and mighty at every stall that it beckons me. I never ate it growing up, so I had to learn to like it. I have. I can even say I love it. My girlfriend Kathleen puts it in her green salads year round—fantastic. Naturally, my favorite fennel recipe is a slaw. Add some vinegar, sugar, and mustard to just about anything, and I'm happy. Give fennel a chance. It's way better than anything else with a licorice flavor.

Prep time: 15 to 20 minutes
Serves 4 to 6

1 garlic clove, minced
1/4 teaspoon sea salt
2 tablespoons cider vinegar
3 tablespoons extra-virgin olive oil
1/4 teaspoon freshly ground pepper
1/4 teaspoon ground coriander
1 teaspoon sugar
2 teaspoons Dijon mustard
Zest and juice of 1 orange
1 large fennel bulb, core removed and shaved on a mandoline
1 tablespoon chopped fennel fronds
1/2 cup shaved red onion
3 tablespoons minced Italian parsley leaves (about 1 bunch)
2 tablespoons capers, optional

In a medium bowl, whisk together garlic, salt, vinegar, olive oil, pepper, coriander, sugar, mustard, orange zest, and juice. Fold in shaved fennel, fennel fronds, red onion, and parsley. Toss well to distribute the dressing and serve. Preparing this a day in advance helps mellow the fennel.

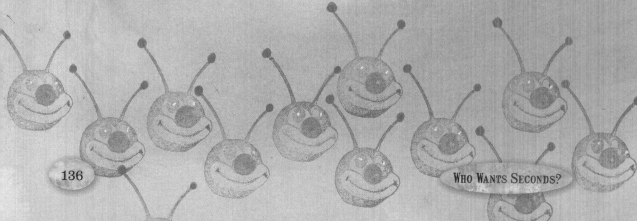

ENDIVE, AVOCADO & POTATO SALAD

We eat a lot of avocados here in California, and this is a simple and sublime celebration of the avocado's greatness. It's just a wonderful, wonderful salad. Enjoy at room temperature.

Prep time: 15 minutes, plus 30 minutes resting time
Cooking time: 10 to 15 minutes
Serves 6 to 8

1 pound waxy-skin potatoes (like Red Bliss), cut into bite-size chunks
1 1/2 tablespoons cider vinegar
1 1/2 tablespoons fresh lemon juice
2 tablespoons minced shallot or onion
1 tablespoon Dijon or Pommery mustard
1/3 cup extra-virgin olive oil

1 teaspoon coarse sea salt
1/2 teaspoon freshly ground pepper
2 Belgian endives, cut into small, salad-size slices
2 ripe avocados, cut into 1/4-inch cubes
1/4 cup diced green onion or chives

Place potatoes in a medium pot of salted water. Bring to a boil, reduce heat, and simmer until potatoes are fork-tender, 10 to 15 minutes.

While potatoes cook, whisk together vinegar, lemon juice, shallot, and mustard in small bowl. Drizzle in the olive oil in a slow, steady stream, whisking constantly until emulsified. Add salt and pepper; taste and add more if desired.

When potatoes are cooked, drain and place them, still warm, in a medium bowl and toss with three-quarters of the vinaigrette. Let stand for 30 minutes. Add endive and avocado just before serving and toss with remaining vinaigrette. Stir in green onion or chives, and crack more fresh pepper on top. Serve at room temperature.

Vegan Caesar
WITH
NU CHEEZE AND HANDMADE CROUTONS

Caesar salad is a classic crowd pleaser. And really, what could be simpler? The cheese, dressing, and croutons can be made ahead of time, and the romaine is easy to cut and dry the day of the party. If you have lots of variety in your meal, one head of romaine lettuce can serve up to 8 people. You'll have a little extra dressing, which you can save to use as a dipping sauce or to drizzle on roasted asparagus.

Prep time: 10 minutes, plus Nu Cheeze and Handmade Croutons
Serves 6 to 8

DRESSING
4 tablespoons vegan cream cheese or vegan mayonnaise
2 garlic cloves, minced
1 tablespoon fresh lemon juice
1 tablespoon cider vinegar
2 tablespoons balsamic vinegar
2 tablespoons diced onion
1 teaspoon freshly ground pepper
1 tablespoon Dijon mustard
1/2 cup extra-virgin olive oil
2 heaping tablespoons capers
Sea salt to taste

SALAD
1 head romaine lettuce, cleaned and torn into pieces
1 cup Handmade Croutons (*see next page*)
1/3 cup Nu Cheeze (*see next page*)

To prepare dressing, place cream cheese, garlic, lemon juice, vinegars, onion, pepper, and mustard in a blender and blend on high until creamy. With the blender on medium, drizzle in olive oil. Add capers, pulsing to combine but not purée. Taste and add salt as needed, in 1/4 teaspoon increments.

Pour 1/2 cup of dressing into a large bowl. Add lettuce and toss well. Add croutons and Nu Cheeze and toss again. Drizzle a little more dressing on top if you like that.

Nu Cheeze

Nutritional yeast is a huge flavor booster for vegan cooking. It has a good deal of umami going on in there, and it really helps to add a little funkability without the fermented fish or dairy in a non-vegan Caesar. Just remember that a little goes a long way. Nutritional yeast is balanced with the seeds in this parmesan-like recipe, but some people use it straight up as a pasta topper.

Prep time: 5 minutes
Makes 2 cups

1/2 cup nutritional yeast
1/2 cup toasted salted sunflower seeds
1/2 cup toasted salted pumpkin seeds
1/2 cup toasted breadcrumbs

Blend all ingredients in a processor or blender until it turns to coarse meal. Refrigerate in an airtight container for up to several months and use any time instead of parmesan.

Handmade Croutons

Really, croutons are simply seasoned toast. There's no need to ever buy them if you have a toaster. Just make a piece of toast, spread it with a little garlic and olive oil, and cut it—there, you have croutons. This is a more sophisticated crouton recipe for a crowd.

Prep time: 10 minutes
Cooking time: 25 minutes
Makes 4 cups

4 cups bread of choice,
   cut into 1/2-inch cubes
1/4 cup extra-virgin olive oil
1 teaspoon dried basil or Italian herbs
1/2 teaspoon granulated onion

1/2 teaspoon granulated garlic
1/2 teaspoon dried thyme
1/2 teaspoon paprika
1/2 teaspoon sea salt
1/4 teaspoon freshly ground pepper

Preheat oven to 350°. Place cubed bread in a large bowl, drizzle with olive oil and toss to coat. In a small bowl, combine basil, onion, garlic, thyme, paprika, salt, and pepper. Sprinkle this herb mixture over the bread and toss to coat evenly. Spread croutons on a rimmed baking sheet in a single layer. Bake for 15 minutes and stir the croutons, then bake until lightly browned and crisp, about 10 more minutes. Allow croutons to cool before serving. Store in an airtight container.

SWEET POTATO LASAGNA

My favorite kind of sweet potato is the Japanese version. It has a yellow flesh, a dry texture, and the flavor of Italian chestnuts. Japanese sweets are delicious in this recipe, but any sweet potato will do. The combination of sweet potatoes, marinara, and noodles is ridiculously satisfying.

Prep time: 20 to 30 minutes
Cooking time: 1 hours, 10 minutes, plus roasting sweet potatoes
Serves 8 to 10

5 tablespoons olive oil, divided
1 small onion, diced
4 garlic cloves, minced
8 ounces mushrooms (any kind), finely diced
1 large red bell pepper, seeded and diced
2 carrots, peeled and diced
3 ribs celery, diced
1/2 teaspoon dried thyme or 2 sprigs fresh
2 bay leaves
1 24-ounce jar marinara sauce
2 teaspoons sugar
1 teaspoon light-colored vinegar
1 cup water
3 roasted sweet potatoes, peeled and cooled (*see recipe page 132*)
1 teaspoon sea salt
1 teaspoon freshly ground pepper
1 16-ounce package lasagna noodles (traditional or no-boil)
3 roma tomatoes, thinly sliced
3 tablespoons toasted breadcrumbs (*see recipe page 37*)
   or Nu Cheeze (*see recipe page 139*)

Preheat oven to 350°. In a large skillet on medium-high heat, add 3 tablespoons olive oil and sauté onion, garlic, mushrooms, red pepper, carrot, celery, thyme, and bay leaves until the vegetables are soft and lightly browned, about 8 minutes. Add marinara, sugar, vinegar, and water and stir to combine. Move to the back burner and simmer over low heat. While it simmers, lightly mash sweet potatoes in a large bowl. Season with salt and pepper, but don't use more than called for.

After about 15 minutes, remove sauce from heat. Assemble lasagna by scantily covering the bottom of a 9" x 13" pan with 1/2 cup sauce. Next, lay out a row of noodles edge to edge in a single layer. Evenly drop about half of the mashed sweet potatoes in large spoonfuls over the noodles; do not spread. Drop 1 cup sauce in spoonfuls, add a second layer of noodles, and press down gently until sauce oozes through the noodle layer. Add remaining sweet potatoes, then 1 1/2 cups sauce and a third layer of noodles. Spread remaining 1 cup sauce over the top. Cover lasagna with thinly sliced tomatoes. Sprinkle breadcrumbs or Nu Cheeze on top and drizzle with 2 tablespoons olive oil.

Cover with foil and bake for 60 minutes, removing foil at 40 minutes to brown the top. The lasagna is done when a knife inserted in the very middle slides in and out easily, ensuring cooked noodles. Let cool 10 to 15 minutes before slicing.

If a vegan is coming to dinner, this lasagna would make them very happy. It's a classic white lasagna with a dairy-free twist. The cashew cream can be made ahead, making assembly a snap.

Prep time: 15 minutes, plus Cashew Cream Sauce, Tofu Crumbles, and Nu Cheeze
Cooking time: 1 hour, 10 minutes
Serves 8 to 10

2 tablespoons olive oil, plus more to drizzle
1 pound mushrooms (any kind), sliced
1 cup diced onion
2 garlic cloves, minced
8 ounces fresh spinach, cleaned and roughly chopped
12 ounces (about 3/4 of a package) lasagna noodles (traditional or no-boil)
1 batch Savory Cashew Cream Sauce (*see recipe next page*)
1 cup Tofu Crumbles (*see recipe page 146*)
1/2 cup Nu Cheeze (*see recipe page 139*)

Preheat oven to 350°. Grease a 9" x 13" baking dish and set aside. In a large skillet over medium-high heat, add olive oil and sauté mushrooms, onion, and garlic until soft, about 8 minutes. Set aside.

To assemble lasagna, pour a scant cup of Cashew Cream Sauce in the bottom of the pan. Cover with 1 layer of lasagna noodles, edge to edge. Top with 1/2 of the spinach, 1/3 of the sautéed mushrooms and onion, and 1/3 of the Tofu Crumbles. Add 2 1/2 cups Cashew Cream Sauce, distributing as evenly as possible. Add second layer of noodles and press down lightly. Add remaining 1/2 of spinach, then 1/3 of mushroom-onion mixture, 1/3 of Tofu Crumbles, and 2 cups sauce. Cover with a layer of noodles, reserving 1 noodle.

On the top layer, add remaining mushroom mixture and Tofu Crumbles. Break up reserved noodle and scatter it on top. Completely cover scattered noodles with remaining 1 1/2 cup sauce. Drizzzle with olive oil and sprinkle with Nu Cheeze. Cover tightly with foil and bake for 50 minutes. Remove foil and continue cooking until golden brown and a knife inserted into the middle comes out easily (ensuring cooked noodles), about 10 minutes.

Savory Cashew Cream Sauce

This is the best sauce for savory foods, especially vegan lasagna and vegan quiche. It makes a fantastic mushroom bread pudding, and it's a great gravy base. It tastes better if you let the cashew mixture soak overnight; just make sure to warm it up before puréeing so it gets smooth.

Prep time: 15 minutes, plus soaking time
Cooking time: About 25 minutes
Makes about 7 cups

3 tablespoons olive oil
2 chopped shallots or 1/2 cup chopped onion
3 garlic cloves, minced
1 cup white wine
2 bay leaves
1 teaspoon minced fresh rosemary
3 sprigs thyme
4 cups rice or other nondairy milk, plus more if needed
1/4 cup nutritional yeast
1 teaspoon sea salt
1/2 teaspoon freshly ground pepper
2 cups whole unsalted cashews, preferably raw
8 ounces tofu

Place large saucepan over medium-high heat, add olive oil, and sauté shallots and garlic until translucent, about 6 minutes. Add wine, bay leaves, rosemary, and thyme and reduce until wine is almost evaporated, another 10 minutes. Add rice milk, nutritional yeast, salt, and pepper and heat until hot but not boiling. Remove from heat. Add cashews and leave them to soak in the warm milk mixture for at least 1 hour or as long as overnight, refrigerated. While still warm (reheat if chilled overnight), remove bay leaves and thyme stems and purée mixture in a powerful blender with the tofu until smooth, drizzling in more milk if needed to make a creamy consistency. If you prefer a super-smooth finished sauce, strain it through a fine-mesh sieve.

BAKED POLENTA MARINARA WITH PESTO AND TOFU CRUMBLES

This recipe keeps coming back at us—everyone loves it. Again, the corn troubles me, but imported polenta from Italy should be GMO free, and that makes me happy. You can prepare all the components in advance, so the final assembly is quick and easy.

Prep time: 35 minutes, plus Vegan Pesto and Tofu Crumbles
Cooking time: 30 minutes
Serves 10

ASSEMBLY

3 cups Quick Polenta (*see recipe next page*)
1 to 2 cups marinara sauce (from a jar)
1 cup Tofu Crumbles (*see recipe page 146*)
1/2 cup Vegan Pesto (*see recipe page 146*)
1/4 cup Nu Cheeze (*see recipe page 139*)
Basil leaves for garnish

Preheat oven to 350°. Place cooked polenta in a greased 9" x 13" baking dish (or perhaps it's already in such a dish) and cover with 1 to 2 cups marinara sauce. Alternately, if you made a loaf of polenta, slice and arrange in a baking pan and cover with marinara. Top with Tofu Crumbles and cook until bubbly, about 30 minutes. Remove from oven, top with generous dollops of Vegan Pesto, sprinkle with Nu Cheeze, garnish with fresh basil, and serve.

QUICK POLENTA

I know it's controversial, but I have no problem with quick polenta. I even like the premade logs—reminds me of cornmeal mush from back in the day.

Prep time: 5 to 10 minutes
Cooking time: about 6 minutes
Makes about 3 cups

3 cups vegetable stock
2 garlic cloves, minced
2 teaspoons chopped fresh herbs
  (rosemary, basil, and/or thyme)

2 tablespoons extra-virgin olive oil
1/2 teaspoon sea salt
3/4 cup instant polenta

In large, heavy saucepan, bring stock, garlic, herbs, olive oil, and salt to boil over high heat. Gradually add cornmeal in a thin stream, whisking until smooth. Reduce heat to low and cook, stirring occasionally, until cornmeal is soft and mixture is thick and creamy, about 6 minutes. Pour into a greased pie pan or 9" x 9" baking pan if you want to slice it. Can be made 1 day ahead.

Prep time: 5 minutes
Makes about 1 cup

2 cups clean and beautiful basil, spinach, and parsley in any combination, stemmed
1/2 cup shelled unsalted nuts in any combination (try pecans and pine nuts)

1 to 3 cloves fresh garlic
1/2 cup extra-virgin olive oil at room temperature
Sea salt

Combine the greens, nuts, and garlic in a food processor and process the mixture until it turns into a coarse meal. Or you can put it all in a mortar and pestle and pound it, although I have never done that. Good luck, I hear it works! With the processor on, drizzle in the olive oil in a steady stream until the mixture gets tight and bright green, like a fluffy, smooth paste. Taste and add salt as you prefer.

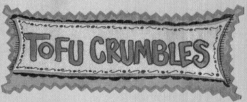

I love these roasted crumbles not just on polenta and pasta but on salads, too. They add a nice texture, and the miso-tahini blend packs a surprisingly delicious punch. I like them cooked until well done, but they are also tasty when golden brown—try them both ways.

Prep time: 30 minutes
Cook time: 30 minutes
Makes about 2 1/2 cups

2 tablespoons tahini
2 tablespoons light-colored miso
1 tablespoon nutritional yeast
1 tablespoon olive oil
1 pound (2 containers) firm tofu

Preheat the oven to 350°. Place tofu bricks in a pie pan in the sink. Put another pie pan on top of the tofu and weight the pan down with a large bottle of water, canned food, or a dumbbell. The water will ooze out of the tofu and reduce the cooking time. (This takes about 30 minutes.) Meanwhile, place tahini, miso, nutritional yeast, and olive oil in a large bowl and mix to combine. When the tofu feels spongy and not so wet, crumble it into tahni mixture. Spread mixture evenly on a rimmed baking sheet and roast until lightly browned, about 30 minutes. (Cook a little longer until darker brown if you like your crumbles darker and crispier.) Allow to cool and use as needed. Store in refrigerator.

Homemade Gingerale

Ginger ale is really fun to brew and falls into the kitchen-chemistry division of the culinary arts. Every time I make it, my friends go wild! I make a few batches around the holidays and a special batch for my friend Marilyn on her birthday. It takes three days from start to fermented finish—a very important part of the timing equation. I've tried it with honey and other sugar substitutes and made nothing but a mess. If it's your first time, I recommend sticking straight with this recipe.

Prep time: 15 minutes, plus Ginger Concentrate and 2 to 3 days for fermenting
Makes 2 liters

1/4 teaspoon Champagne yeast (available at brew stores and online)
2 liters distilled or filtered water
1 cup plus 1/8 teaspoon sugar
1 cup fresh lemon juice
1 quart Ginger Concentrate (*see recipe page 21*)
1 clean 2-liter bottle with a tight-fitting lid, plastic preferred, glass okay (a used 2-liter beverage bottle is ideal)

First, you need to proof the yeast. Combine yeast and 1 cup lukewarm (not hot) water in a small glass or ceramic bowl. Add 1/8 teaspoon sugar. Stir and let sit for 10 minutes. If mixture is a little bubbly, the yeast is good; if not, throw it out, get new yeast, and do it again.

In a small saucepan over medium heat, melt 1 cup sugar and the lemon juice until combined, about 3 minutes. Let cool for a few minutes (super-hot temperatures will kill yeast). Using a funnel, pour lemon mixture, proofed yeast, and Ginger Concentrate into the bottle, swirling until it mixes together well. Add enough water to fill the bottle, leaving at least 2 inches at the top for expansion. Screw on the cap, give it a good shake, and leave it on the counter.

In 6 hours or so, the fermentation will be starting. Burp the bottle (open the cap a little to relieve the pressure). At this point, the ale shouldn't squirt all over the place, but in another 8 hours, you should do this over the sink. Burp every 6 to 8 hours, or at the very least, morning and night. On the morning of the third day, it's ready. Give it a final burp and refrigerate. Refrigeration stops the fermentation process.

Roasted Salt and Pepper Vegetables

Whatever the season, whatever the vegetable, just crank up the oven, fill two large baking sheets with vegetables, and roast. This should be the first item on every menu. EAT MORE VEGETABLES! This recipe makes it easy.

Prep time: 10 minutes
Cooking time: 40 minutes
Serves 4 to 8

3 pounds brussels sprouts, green
   beans, romenesco, and/or
   zucchini, in any combination
1/4 cup green olive oil
Sea salt and freshly ground
   pepper to taste

Preheat oven to 400°. Remove tough outer leaves and bottoms from brussels sprouts. Trim other vegetables into uniformly sized chunks, removing stem ends. In a large bowl, toss one of the vegetables with a drizzle of olive oil and sprinkling of salt and pepper, then repeat for all others, one at a time. Spread them in a single layer on 1 to 2 rimmed baking sheets, keeping them separate. Roast for 30 minutes, then check and remove any cooked vegetables and flip over the ones that still need cooking. Green beans should be done at 30 minutes; zucchini takes 35 to 40 minutes; brussels sprouts need 45 to 50.

You can add back the zucchini and green beans for a few minutes to reheat, or serve them all at room temperature. Make a pretty platter, consider drizzling with Balsamic Vinaigrette (page 73) or Boozy Blackberry Balsamic (page 133), and enjoy!

onion bhaji

I love onions and want others to love them, too. If your people are onion phobic, tone down these little onion fritters with shredded carrot or zucchini, but keep pushing the onions, because alliums need more love. Have you heard the one where you put onions in your socks and go to bed and it'll clear up congestion? That's pretty special.

Typically, a bhaji is made with garbanzo bean (chickpea) flour. It's in Middle Eastern or Indian grocers and is labeled garam, gram, or besan flour. (You can also look for Bob's Red Mill, a brand now at Whole Foods and other health food stores.) I have found masa to be a fine substitute for chickpea flour.

Prep time: 30 minutes
Cooking time: About 25 minutes
Makes about 10 pieces

1 large sweet or white onion, halved and thinly sliced (about 2 cups)
1/2 teaspoon sea salt
2 garlic cloves, minced
1 teaspoon turmeric
2 teaspoons curry powder
1/2 teaspoon freshly ground pepper
2 tablespoons minced cilantro
3/4 cup garbanzo bean flour or masa
1 teaspoon baking soda
1 cup olive oil for frying
Water, if needed
1 lemon, cut into wedges for serving

Place onion slices in a bowl, sprinkle with salt, and mix well with your hands to separate the slices. Mix in garlic, turmeric, curry powder, pepper, and cilantro. Stir in the garbanzo bean flour or masa and baking soda, and continue to mix by hand. If the dough seems too thick to mix, add water, 1 teaspoon at a time, until a soft dough forms. The final result is mostly onion with dough binding them.

Heat 3 tablespoons oil in a deep frying pan over high heat. Drop the dough by tablespoons in small batches into the hot oil and fry until golden, 2 to 3 minutes on each side. (They can also be pan-fried in a nonstick skillet.) Remove to a plate. Serve hot or at room temperature with additional salt and lemon wedges.

Make It and Take It

Every year, on the Sunday before Thanksgiving, we have a crazy pie-making flash-mob party at Jennie Cooks called Make It & Take It. We open our doors at 11 a.m., and everybody makes holiday pies until dinnertime. We serve a nice vegan-friendly lunch and get some local beer from our friends at Eagle Rock Brewery. Triple Chicken Foot keeps the mood lively with their old-time string band, picking tunes all afternoon. We bake more than 100 pies that day, and there's no rush. The ovens must open hundreds of times, affecting the temperature; flour is *everywhere*; and we give children knives. It's a little crazy, and it's certainly our most memorable event of the year. Families come, couples come, single men and women come.

The week before, my baker makes about 150 vegan pie crusts and freezes them. We get the recipes and ingredients ready so people can make pumpkin, pecan, and/or local apple pies in either vegan or traditional varieties. We get out the fancy little cookie cutters for crust decorating, and enthusiastic bakers adorn pies for their holiday celebrations. It has turned into a tradition for many families. When the crazy is done, it's great to look back at all the first-time bakers who come in a little timid and leave with their first pie!

A Pie Tradition

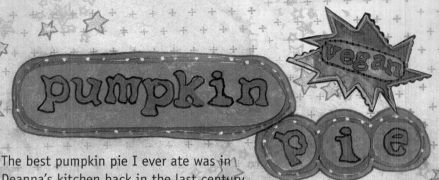

pumpkin pie
vegan

The best pumpkin pie I ever ate was in
Deanna's kitchen back in the last century.
Since then it's fallen out of favor with
me—after all, it's a vegetable, so what's it doing in a pie? While I believe it makes
a far better breakfast than a dessert, this vegan pumpkin pie is creamy and delicious
anytime. The recipe makes two; you can cut it in half for one.

Prep time: 15 minutes
Cooking time: About 1 1/2 hours
Makes 2 pies

1 cup cooked pumpkin or other winter squash
16 ounces (2 containers) vegan cream cheese,
    room temperature
1/4 cup flour
1 teaspoon ground ginger
2 teaspoons ground cinnamon
1/2 teaspoon ground nutmeg
1/2 teaspoon sea salt
3/4 cup firmly packed brown sugar

1/4 cup sugar
3 tablespoons orange juice
Zest of 1 orange
1 tablespoon vanilla extract
2 pie crusts, fit into 9-inch tart
    pans (*see recipe page 186, or
    use pre-made crusts*); if crusts
    are homemade, par bake them
    first (*see page 187*)

Preheat oven to 325°. In a large bowl or stand mixer with whisk attachment, mix
together pumpkin, cream cheese, and flour. Add ginger, cinnamon, nutmeg, salt,
sugars, orange juice, zest, and vanilla and whisk mixture until very smooth (no
lumps allowed!). Pour into pie shells and bake until the centers look firm, 50 to 60
minutes. Turn oven off and let pies cool in the oven 25 minutes to further firm up
the pie filling.

whipped cream

At the Shoppe, we're big fans of Mimic Cream. It's a soy-free, nut-based whippable
topping that is dairy free and delicious. It's available in natural food stores in the
refrigerator section.

Coconut Almond Whoopie Pies

Whoopie pies are a Pennsylvania favorite on the prowl for renewed attention; I've updated them here to make them vegan. The cake is soft and dry at first, but it moistens as it sits with the creamy filling. It's a perfect lunchbox treat and a great party favor. Try to make the cakey cookies around the same size so the sandwiches are properly sized.

Prep time: 1 hour
Cooking time: 10 minutes
Makes 14 sandwich cookies

COOKIES

3/4 cups almond milk
1/2 coconut milk, cream reserved
1 teaspoon cider vinegar
1/2 cup vegan butter
1/2 cup sugar
1/4 cup brown sugar
1 tablespoon vanilla extract
2 cups all-purpose flour
3/4 cup cocoa powder, sifted
1 teaspoon baking soda
1 teaspoon baking powder
1 teaspoon sea salt

BUTTERCREAM FILLING

1/2 cup vegan butter
2 cups confectioners sugar
1 tablespoon vanilla extract
1 teaspoon almond extract
2 tablespoons resevrved coconut cream
1/2 cup ground almonds, divided
1/2 cup flaked coconut, divided

Preheat oven to 350°. To make cookies, whisk together almond milk, coconut milk, and vinegar in a small bowl and set aside to curdle. Grease 2 large baking sheets.

Using an electric mixer, cream together butter, sugar, brown sugar, and vanilla until flluffy. Scrape the sides of the mixing bowl with a spatula. Add flour, cocoa, baking soda, baking powder, salt, and curdled milk. Mix on low, scraping down the sides of the bowl, until just combined. Drop batter by rounded tablespoons onto greased baking sheets, allowing room to spread. Moisten your fingers with water and lightly press on the dough. Make them uniform so both sides of the sandwich match, and not too big because everyone gets 2 cookies in one serving. Bake until cookies puff up in the middle, 10 to 12 minutes, rotating the pan at 7 minutes.

While they bake, make the buttercream filling. Using an electric mixer, cream together vegan butter, sugar, vanilla, almond extract, and coconut cream until fluffy. Stir in 1/4 cup each of almonds and coconut, reserving the other 1/4 cup to garnish the edges of the sandwich cookies. Chill buttercream at least 1 hour (but not overnight—it's easier to work with on the same day).

When cool (about 15 minutes), make sandwiches with 2 cookies and a generous scoop of buttercream, about 1 1/2 tablespoons. Squeeze the filling to the ends of the cookies and roll the exposed buttercream in the ground almonds and coconut for garnish. Wrap individually and chill for up to 3 days.

A Balanced Dinner Party Table

One of my favorite jobs is menu planning. I relish the opportunity to expand the food horizons of the general public, and I love trying out new recipes on my friends. They're a hearty bunch that graciously eats whatever I make. I love that about them. They so appreciate the goodness in the greens, and they make me proud of what I do.

The best way to create a balanced table is to plan the meal around seasonal vegetables. I start almost every dinner with a green salad and crusty bread. In the cooler months, I serve a cup of soup, too. I build the meal around at least two vegetables, one green and one orange or red, and I keep all dishes vegan except for the meat. I serve two entrées, one meat and one vegan, but if you're a beginner, one is fine. Serving guests lots of local produce feels fantastic, so plan a trip to the farmers' market to coincide with the party. I always do a full pass on the market to see what's bursting forth before I make my selections. Farmers' market produce tends to last longer than the supermarket kind, so you can shop earlier in the week and avoid last-minute stress. Look for bright white cut marks on the vegetables for maximum freshness. It's also a good idea to make soups, sauces, and dressings a few days ahead. Food lasts longer than we think once refrigerated, and it often improves with age.

Making the Fruit Crumble in jars (*see page 87*) is a simple presentation that delivers a wow factor. They can be prepared ahead of time and baked while you're eating dinner—or better yet, have them baking when guests arrive. The smell of a cinnamon fruit crumble in the oven is a heartwarming welcome that sets up a deliciously sweet evening.

Chapter
Seven
SUNDAY
SUPPERS

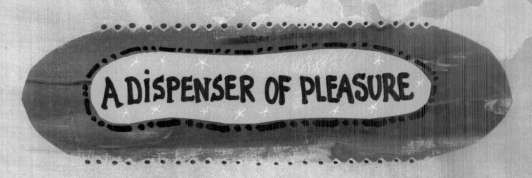

A DISPENSER OF PLEASURE

After almost 30 years in this whack hospitality business, I can safely say that I could not have done it alone. My family, my friends, and my amazing staff share in my success. It's been a community project.

Our knowledge of food in America, and how it can heal and change us, is finally in the forefront of the news. Community is a huge part of the equation. It's all about connection, and food is one of the best ways to expand neighborly reach. My friend Tom calls it the GPS system: Grow, Prepare, Share. My Uncle Bill called it the 3F foundation to life: Friendship, Family, and Farming.

Whatever you want to call it, there's a spiritual connection that comes from sharing food. It helps build healthy relationships and creates a loving environment. It lingers in the air.

When I embrace my hospitality prowess and approach the world as a willing servant working toward a greater good, I am at my best. I am reminded that I can quit my job but I cannot quit my calling. I am called to serve...food.

I have always been inspired by MLK's quote on service: "Everybody can be great...because anybody can serve. You don't have to have a college degree to serve. You don't have to make your subject and verb agree to serve. You only need a heart full of grace. A soul generated by love."

One of the best parts of being a caterer for life is that I can hold the space for others to come together. Perhaps it's my superpower. It keeps me creative, communicative, and grateful. What a great job I have: I'm a dispenser of pleasure.

I live for my next meal with my family and friends. When we get together, I feel loved and appreciated. We laugh and eat and laugh. It heals me. I wake up the next day with a song in my heart and a smile on my face. A little love in the kitchen goes a very long way.

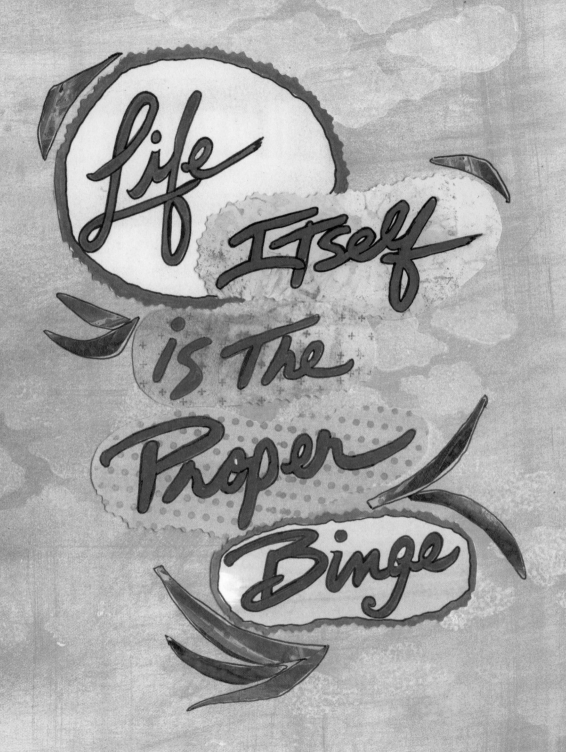

Life Itself is The Proper Binge

MASALA CHAI

Chai means "tea"! This is a tasty warm beverage to serve during chilly weather. Add a shot of whiskey or Amaretto and call it a chai toddy. To make it vegan, leave out the milk and serve your milk alternative on the side, so it doesn't curdle.

Prep time: 5 minutes
Cooking time: 15 minutes
Makes 1 quart (about 6 servings)

6 cups water
10 whole green cardamom pods, smashed
1 large knob (about 4 ounces) unpeeled ginger, sliced into coins
4 3-inch cinnamon sticks
2 star anise

10 cloves
2 teaspoons whole black peppercorns
2 cups milk
4 black tea bags
1/4 to 1/2 cup sugar or preferred sweetener, to taste

In a soup pot, combine water, cardamom, ginger, cinnamon sticks, star anise, cloves, peppercorns, milk, and tea. Bring the mixture to a boil, then lower the heat and simmer for a few minutes until the mixture is fragrant. Remove from heat and let steep 10 minutes. Strain out tea leaves and seasonings. Add sweetener to taste.

Naturally, this flavored vodka is best made in blackberry season and left to ferment until the fall. The color is gorgeous. Combined with equal parts soda water and a wedge of lime, it makes a stunning signature cocktail. Save the strained berries to serve atop ice cream!

Prep time: 15 minutes, plus 1 month waiting
Makes 2 quarts

3 cups blackberries
3/4 cup sugar
Juice of 1/2 lemon
1 750 ML bottle vodka
1 2-quart jar with a wide mouth and tight-fitting lid

Wash blackberries and leave them whole. (Smashing the berries results in a cloudier finished product.) Fill 2-quart jar with blackberries and sugar and shake gently until well combined and a syrup starts to develop. Squeeze in the lemon juice, top off the jar with vodka, and seal the lid. Wrap the bottle in dark cloth or stash in a dark place for 1 month. This step is crucial for the best flavor and color. After 1 month, strain and transfer to a serving bottle. Serve chilled over ice or mixed with seltzer or lemonade—fantastic.

VARIATION:
This works well for any kind of berry or stone fruit.
Don't smash the fruit if you like a clear vodka.

Minted Lamb Meatballs

Lamb is a nice alternative to beef, and it's readily available at many farmers' markets from local ranchers. Give it a go, and before you know it, you might even experiment with goat. Try new things!

Also: This is a wonderful tomato sauce that works with all sorts of things, from pasta or polenta to sausage or chicken. Experiment!

Prep time: 20 to 30 minutes
Cooking time: 20 to 25 minutes
Serves 6 to 8

1 1/2 pounds ground lamb
1/4 cup ground almonds
1/4 cup breadcrumbs
5 tablespoons chopped fresh mint, divided
2 cloves garlic, minced, divided
2 teaspoons ground cumin
1/2 teaspoon ground cinnamon
1 teaspoon sea salt, divided
1/4 teaspoon freshly ground pepper
1/4 cup olive oil, divided
1 onion, chopped
2 cups (or 1 15-ounce can) crushed tomatoes in thick purée
2 teaspoons honey or sugar
2 teaspoons balsamic vinegar
1 cinnamon stick
Grated orange zest for garnish

In a large bowl, combine lamb, almonds, breadcrumbs, 3 tablespoons mint, half the garlic, 1 teaspoon cumin, 1/2 teaspoon salt, cinnamon, and pepper. Mix thoroughly and shape the mixture into 24 or so small meatballs, about the size of a ping-pong ball. You can also make them smaller if you're making this as an appetizer.

In a large skillet, heat 2 tablespoons oil over medium-high heat. Add meatballs and cook, turning, until browned, about 5 minutes. Set aside.

In the same pan, heat the remaining 2 tablespoons oil over moderate heat. Add onion and remaining garlic and cook, stirring occasionally, until translucent, about 5 minutes. Add crushed tomatoes, honey, balsamic vinegar, cinnamon stick, remaining 1 teaspoon cumin, and 1/2 teaspoon salt. Bring to a boil, reduce heat to a simmer, cover, and cook for 10 minutes. Add meatballs to the tomato sauce and continue simmering, covered, until the meatballs are cooked through, another 10 minutes (less time if you made small ones). Stir in remaining 2 tablespoons mint, sprinkle with orange zest, and serve.

VARIATION: If you like a softer meatball, skip the browning stage. Cook the sauce first and add the raw meatballs to the sauce. Cover and simmer until an internal instant meat thermometer reads 160 degrees, about 20 minutes.

Chicken Cacciatore

This is the dreamiest dinner, especially when served on fat pappardelle noodles. The carrots make it a little sweet, and the sausage gives it depth. Add some Spinach for a Crowd (*see page 175*) and a baguette and call the neighbors—party at your house. Do it.

Prep time: 15 to 20 minutes
Cooking time: 50 to 55 minutes
Serves 6 to 8

3 tablespoons olive oil
8 ounces mushrooms (any variety), sliced
2 cups chopped onion
1 teaspoon Italian herbs
2 bay leaves
2 thyme sprigs or 1/2 teaspoon dried
4 cloves garlic, minced
1 pound Italian link sausage (chicken or pork)
4 bone-in chicken thighs (about 1 pound), skin removed
4 large carrots, peeled and cut into 1-inch logs
2 teaspoons chopped fresh rosemary
1 cup dry red wine
2 cups fresh or canned diced tomatoes, with juice
2 cups marinara sauce (from a jar is fine)
1 tablespoon balsamic vinegar
2 tablespoons drained capers
1 teaspoon sugar, if needed
1/3 cup chopped or ripped basil

Heat oil in a large skillet over medium heat. Add mushrooms and onion and sauté until the onion turns translucent, about 8 minutes. Add Italian herbs, bay leaves, thyme, and garlic and sauté another minute. Add whole sausages and brown on all sides. Remove sausage with slotted spoon and set aside.

In the same skillet, increase heat to high and add chicken thighs skin side down first (even though the skin has been removed). Keep the thighs from touching while cooking, so the meat will sear properly. Sear on both sides. Once they are brown, add carrots, rosemary, and red wine and deglaze the pan, either working around the chicken or pushing it to the side of the pan. Once the tasty bits from the bottom of the pan are in the wine mixture, add diced tomatoes and marinara. When it starts to bubble, reduce heat to a simmer. Cut each sausage link into 4 pieces and drop it in the stew. It's okay if it's raw in the middle, it'll cook in the cacciatore. Simmer, uncovered, for 40 minutes, stirring every 10 minutes and scraping the bottom. Add vinegar and capers. Taste the sauce—if it's a little sharp, add 1 teaspoon sugar (but the carrots should lend plenty of sweet). Garnish with basil and serve with gusto.

Pasta Alla Checca

Checca, a classic chop of tomato, basil, and garlic, is California comfort food. We get heirloom tomatoes 9 months out of the year here in L.A. (Yes, I'm bragging.) They're grown outside on organic family farms, and they just keep coming. This sauce is *à la minoot* and very lightly cooked. Fresh tomato sauce is a must-have recipe for every chef's repertoire. Make it on the full moon, when basil is said to have extra romantic powers, and serve the pasta with a green salad.

Prep time: 10 minutes
Cooking time: 15 minutes, including pasta cooking time
Serves 4 to 6

1 pound pasta of your choice
2 1/2 pounds fresh tomatoes, Italian or heirloom preferred, cut into hearty chunks
1 tablespoon cornstarch
4 cloves garlic, minced
3 tablespoons olive oil
1 teaspoon sea salt
2 teaspoons sugar
2 teaspoons balsamic vinegar
1/2 cup coarsely chopped or torn basil
Grated parmesan or Nu Cheeze (*see page 139*), to taste

Cook the pasta in a large pot of boiling salted water until just barely al dente. Set aside a cup of pasta water, then drain and set pasta aside while you make the checca.

To velvetize the tomatoes, place them in a large bowl, sprinkle on cornstarch, add 1/4 cup pasta water, and stir to combine. Place a large skillet over high heat, add olive oil, and heat until almost smoking. Add garlic and give it a quick stir, avoiding any browning. Add velveted tomatoes (with liquid) and stir to combine. Add salt, sugar, and balsamic vinegar and stir again. Bring sauce to a boil and cook for 2 minutes, stirring occasionally. If the sauce is too thick, thin with additional pasta water. Add cooked pasta, stir to combine, and toss with the basil. Serve with parmesan or Nu Cheeze on the side.

WONDERFUL KALE WALDORF

I created this updated Waldorf salad to keep the Waldorf love alive for all, including vegans. The massaging process makes the kale softer and more flavorful. It's a dish that screams with earthy winter flavors and goodness. Even without the mayonnaise.

Prep time: 20 minutes
Serves 6 to 8

1 bunch kale (about 1 pound)
1 teaspoon soy sauce or tamari
1 teaspoon sugar or maple syrup
1 teaspoon freshly grated ginger
2 tablespoons cider or other light-colored vinegar
2 tablespoons olive oil
1/2 teaspoon freshly ground pepper
1/2 teaspoon sea salt
1/2 cup toasted walnuts
1/2 cup dried fruit (raisins, cranberries and/or sliced dates)
2 ribs celery, cut into thin slices
2 unpeeled apples, cut into fork-friendly pieces

Wash and dry kale, strip the leaves from the ribs, and tear into salad-size pieces. Place in a large bowl. In a small bowl, stir together soy, sugar, grated ginger, vinegar, oil, pepper, and salt and pour mixture over kale. With clean hands, firmly massage and crush the greens to work in the flavoring, as if you're looking for a treasure in the sand at the beach. Stop when the kale is softer, a little darker, and somewhat shiny, about 2 minutes. Toss with walnuts, dried fruit, celery, and apple. Serve the same day, or you can allow the flavors to mingle in the refrigerator for up to 4 days.

Feijoada

Mostly, feijoada is fantastic because it's fun to say. Fedge-wah-dah. It's Brazilian. I hear everyone in Brazil puts their own cheftastic spin on this dish. I love the sweet potatoes and the pineapple in this recipe, and I think black beans are the tops. (Do people say "the tops" anymore?) It should be served as a juicy stew or over rice. The original recipe has pork shoulder in the pot, but as an alternative you can roast some pork and serve it on the side, or make it just as I have here for a plant-based flavor sensation. I served this at my 48th birthday party and the crowd went wild.

Prep time: 30 minutes
Cooking time: About 3 hours
Serves 10 to 12

4 tablespoons olive oil, divided
2 cloves garlic, minced
2 teaspoons minced fresh ginger, plus 1 teaspoon extra for pineapple, if desired
1 medium green pepper, seeded and diced
1 small jalapeño, diced, seeds removed for less heat (wash your hands after)
1 medium onion, diced (about 1 cup)
1 teaspoon dried thyme, or 4 sprigs fresh
2 teaspoons ground cumin
1 cinnamon stick, about 3 inches long
1 1/2 pounds uncooked dried black beans, picked over for rocks and dirt
    (optional to soak overnight in water)
4 cups water
1 teaspoon cider (or other light-colored) vinegar
1 teaspoon red pepper flakes, divided
1 fresh pineapple peeled, cored, and chopped into salsa-size pieces
2 teaspoons sugar
1 medium sweet potato, peeled and uncooked, cut into bite-size chunks
1 28-ounce can diced tomatoes with juice
2 teaspoons sea salt
Zest and juice from 1 orange
1/4 cup coarsely chopped cilantro
1 lime, cut into wedges

Heat 3 tablespoons olive oil in a large soup pot with a heavy bottom. Add garlic, ginger, pepper, jalapeño, onion, thyme, cumin, and cinnamon stick and cook over medium heat, stirring occasionally, until onion is soft, about 7 minutes. Stir in black beans. Add water and vinegar to the pot and bring to a boil over medium-high heat. Reduce heat to a simmer and cook until beans are soft, up to 2 hours, stirring occasionally and scraping the bottom of the pot. If you soaked the beans, start checking for doneness at 60 minutes, then at 15-minute intervals.

While beans are cooking, make the pineapple relish. In a large skillet, swirl in 1 tablespoon olive oil and heat to medium-high. Add ginger, if you're using it, and pineapple chunks. Sprinkle with sugar and 1/2 teaspoon chile flakes. Cook over high heat until the pineapple caramelizes and turns golden brown, about 6 minutes. Set aside in a small bowl.

When beans are soft, add sweet potato and tomatoes and cook until the sweet potato is soft, about 30 minutes. Add salt, remaining 1/2 teaspoon chile flakes, orange juice, and zest. Serve in bowls topped with pineapple relish and chopped cilantro, with a wedge of lemon or lime for garnish.

Slow Roasted Kalua Pork

Pork shoulder (or butt) is great for a party, but it's a little difficult to procure sustainably without buying the whole pig. Talk to your farmer in advance and ask for the whole cut from his next harvest, and you can store it in your freezer until party time. This recipe is meant for a large piece of shoulder, and the seasoning only flavors the outer crust, so you'll want to serve it with a sauce or salsa. It's easy to make, and a little goes a long way, especially if you're serving it SoCal style—in tacos, with salsa and the cabbage slaw we call *curtido*.

Prep time: 10 minutes
Cooking time: 5 hours
Serves 14 to 20

10 cloves garlic, minced
4 coin-size ginger slices, unpeeled, cut into matchsticks
1 1/2 tablespoons dried oregano
1/4 cup soy sauce

2 tablespoons cider or white-wine vinegar
2 tablespoons fresh lemon juice
1 7- to 8-pound bone-in or out pork shoulder (butt), with or without skin

Preheat oven to 350° and place rack in the middle. In a large pan, big enough to hold the roast, place a large piece of foil on the bottom, enough to wrap the pork butt completely. Criss-cross two pieces if necessary. You can also use a large roaster with a tight lid.

Mix garlic, ginger, oregano, soy sauce, vinegar, and lemon juice in a small bowl. Place the pork on the foil. Pour marinade over pork and wrap it up in a tight package, using more foil if needed to completely encase the pork. Place in the oven and roast for 5 hours. Check after 4 hours, and add 2 cups water if the leaking pork juices are getting charred. Once the meat gives when pushed, it's ready. It should be flaky and soft, and it will certainly be delicious. Serve with your favorite sauce and lime wedges. Great for sliders, tacos, or with teriyaki and a side of slaw.

SPINACH FOR A CROWD

People love getting spinach as a side dish, and I like to oblige.
I always serve this dish when I entertain at my house. I have
a large two-oven range and plenty of pans, so I can do massive
batches *à la minoot*. (That's what we chefs say when we're cooking
it up fresh.) It's important to wash your spinach again, no matter
what the bag or the farmer says, to remove that nasty spinach grit.
Have the garlic ready, and this dish cooks in less than 8 minutes.
There are no measurements—you can ballpark this depending on
how many you're feeding.

Prep time: 5 minutes
Cooking time: About 6 minutes

1/4 to 1/2 pound per person super-clean spinach
    (Bloomsdale heirloom spinach if you can find it)
Minced garlic (1 clove per 2 people)
Olive oil
Sea salt to taste

Preheat oven to 400°. Fill a large roasting pan with spinach.
Sprinkle on the garlic and drizzle with olive oil, generously or
sparingly according to your inner chef. Toss with your hands if you
like, but you don't have to. Roast for 4 minutes. Rotate the pan in
the oven and turn the spinach with tongs to distribute the heat
and the flavors. Then return to the oven for another 2 to 4 minutes,
depending on your preference and how much is in there. It's hard
to overcook, but beware, it'll keep shrinking. It's done when some
of the leaves are just wilting. Salt lightly before serving and enjoy
immediately.

ARUGULA, WINTER SQUASH & MEYER LEMON

This simple, elegant salad is beautiful to look at and delightful to eat. Orange-skinned kabocha or delicata squash (both have edible skin) are excellent choices, and the ever-popular butternut is a good safety. The baked squash should be room temperature or warm. If you prepared it ahead of time, give it a minute in the oven to take the chill off. It softens the flesh and improves the flavor. If you don't feel inspired to make the Pickled Cranberries, pomegranate seeds are a nice substitute.

Prep time: 20 minutes
Cooking time: 30 to 40 minutes
Serves 6 to 8

1 winter squash (about 1 1/2 pounds), peeled, seeded, and cut into 1-inch cubes
2 tablespoons extra-virgin olive oil
2 cloves garlic, minced
1/2 teaspoon sea salt, divided
3/4 teaspoon freshly ground pepper, divided
1 bunch (about 12 ounces) local arugula (the packaged stuff doesn't taste nearly as good)
Juice of 1 Meyer lemon
1/2 cup Pickled Cranberries (*see recipe next page*)
1 Meyer lemon, cut into wedges

Preheat oven to 400°. In a large bowl, toss winter squash with olive oil and garlic. Season with 1/4 teaspoon salt and 1/4 teaspoon pepper. Arrange coated squash on a rimmed baking sheet and roast until squash is tender and lightly browned, 30 to 40 minutes. You may make this a day ahead as long as you bring it to room temperature or slightly warm just before serving.

At serving time, toss arugula and winter squash in a large bowl with lemon juice. Add remaining 1/4 teaspoon salt and 1/2 teaspoon pepper and toss well. Platter and garnish with Pickled Cranberries and lemon wedges.

Pickled Cranberries

This was the revelation of the winter of 2012. My hubs Johnny and I were having dinner at our local spot, The Park, and they served a salad with pickled cranberries. Where had you been all my life? I'll never have those overly sweet holiday cranberries again. These are a fantastic addition to so many dishes: in salads, with roasted vegetables or meats, or studding a rice dish.

Prep time: 15 minutes
Cooking time: 8 minutes
Makes 3 cups

3 cups fresh cranberries (1 bag)
3/4 cup cider vinegar
3/4 cup sugar
2 cinnamon sticks, about 3 inches long
2 coin-size ginger slices, about 1/4-inch thick
1/2 teaspoon grated nutmeg
1/2 teaspoon ground clove
1/2 teaspoon coarsely cracked black peppercorns

Wash cranberries and pick over for any stems or bad berries. Set aside.

Combine vinegar and sugar in a medium saucepan and bring to a boil over high heat. Add cinnamon sticks, ginger coins, nutmeg, clove, and peppercorns and return to the boil. Once brine is boiling vigorously, add cranberries. Stir to combine and cook until about 1/3 of the berries have split, 5 to 7 minutes. This is a quick process—overcook the berries and it quickly becomes a relish. Allow to cool and pick out the cinnamon sticks and ginger coins. Store in a jar with a fitted lid; they'll keep in the refrigerator almost indefinitely. An extra treat: The juice is great in salad dressings.

CAULIFLOWER CHIVE LATKES

These are a fantastic and clever alternative to potato latkes. Make sure to cook the cauliflower until it's mashable.

Prep time: 20 minutes
Cooking time: About 12 minutes
Makes about 10 3-inch latkes

1 1/2 pounds cauliflower (1 average head), cut into florets
1/4 cup chopped chives
2 cloves garlic, minced
1 cup breadcrumbs, plus more if needed
2 tablespoons Pommery-style (grainy) mustard
1/2 teaspoon baking powder
3/4 teaspoon sea salt
1/2 teaspoon cayenne or other spicy pepper
1/2 teaspoon freshly ground pepper
2 large eggs, slightly beaten, or 1/2 cup egg substitute
2 to 4 tablespoons olive oil

Bring a large pot of salted water to boil and add cauliflower. Cook until completely soft and tender, 5 to 7 minutes. Drain and return cauliflower to pan. Using 2 metal spatulas or knives, chop cauliflower until it looks like chunky rice. Mix in chives, garlic, breadcrumbs, mustard, baking powder, salt, cayenne, pepper, and eggs. The batter should be stiff enough to make patties with your hands. Add more breadcrumbs if it doesn't hold together well enough.

In a large skillet over medium-high heat, heat 2 tablespoons oil and drop the batter by tablespoons into the pan. Flatten slightly with a spatula and brown for 2 minutes, then flip and cook the other side. Serve with sautéed apples or a delicious sauce of your choosing.

Allison's Cookies

I've been making this particular chocolate chip cookie since I was barefoot and pregnant with my firstborn, Allison, back in 1985. I made it every single night. Does that sound excessive? (I was perfecting the recipe, and we all know that practice makes perfect.)

The key to a crispy edge and a chewy center is in packing the brown sugar when measuring, making sure the butter and eggs are at room temperature, and not over-mixing. A hand mixer or even just stirring with a wooden spoon is best. If you're using a stand mixer, use the paddle and just mix to combine after you add the flour.

Prep time: about 15 minutes
Cooking time: 10 minutes
Makes about 30 cookies

1 cup (2 sticks) butter, at room temperature
1 1/2 cups firmly packed brown sugar
1/2 cup sugar
2 teaspoon vanilla extract
2 eggs, at room temperature
2 1/2 cups all-purpose flour
1 teaspoon baking soda
1 teaspoon sea salt
2 cups good-quality chocolate chips or chunks

Preheat oven to 350°. In a large bowl, cream together butter, brown and white sugar, and vanilla until smooth. Add eggs and beat until fluffy and well combined. Sift flour, baking soda, and salt right on top of the creamed mixture. Stir until combined well and add the chips.

Drop dough onto a greased baking sheet with a tablespoon, allowing room to spread. Bake for about 10 minutes, rotating the baking sheet after 6 minutes. They should look a tad undercooked in the middle, and the edges should be golden brown. Leave them to cool for 2 minutes on the pan, and then use a wide spatula to move them to a plate or cooling rack. There's no need to re-grease the baking sheet after the first batch.

FUNNY CAKE

I resurrected this classic Pennsylvania Dutch breakfast cake/pie hybrid to serve as dessert at our simple suppers. Mostly I like to say the name: Funny Cake! It's funny because you pour the chocolate over and around the cake and it seeps down and bakes into a solid layer of fudge at the bottom. Hilarious, right? If you like a golden-brown finish, you can also pour the chocolate in first, but I like the mottled dark cocoa finish, because it's a mouthwatering setup to the fudgy bottom. This is a great cake/pie to share, because the recipe makes two.

True confessions: I use store-bought pie crusts. But feel free to bust out a handmade flaky shell (see the recipe on page 186)—either is equally scrumptious in the end.

Prep time: 30 minutes
Cooking time: 40 minutes
Makes 2 cakes, each serving 6 to 8

Components
Cake Batter
Chocolate Fudge Syrup
2 8" pie shells, unbaked

Preheat oven to 375° while you make the batter.

CAKE BATTER
2/3 cup butter, at room temperature
2 cups sugar
1 tablespoon vanilla extract
2 eggs
3 cups flour
1 cup milk
1 tablespoon baking powder

Cream together butter, sugar, and vanilla with an electric mixer until smooth. Add eggs, one at a time, beating after each addition. Add flour, milk, and baking powder and mix until combined, scraping down the sides of the bowl once. Set aside while you make the chocolate syrup.

CHOCOLATE FUDGE SYRUP
1 cup hot water
3/4 cup cocoa powder
1 1/2 cups sugar
1 tablespoon vanilla extract

In a large bowl, mix everything together and whisk until well blended and the consistency of a thin sauce.

Assembly

Place pie shells in greased pie pans and crimp the edges to make them as high as possible. Divide the cake batter equally and pour into the 2 shells. Pour the chocolate syrup over the batter and around the edges.

Carefully set the pies on a baking sheet (to catch any gooey chocolate overspill) and bake until a toothpick comes out clean and the top cracks (the chocolate will be bubbling through as well), 35 to 40 minutes.

Useful Information

Menu Planning

It's not easy to come up with clever meal ideas every day, so I say lead with your strengths. If you have a dish you make exceptionally well and people love it, make it whenever you can. No need to fix what's working. I make some mental notes on what's abundant at the market, and then I cruise around the interwebs for ideas... or use this handy cookbook. Themes are always popular—everyone loves an old-fashioned barbecue or taco night. Breakfast for dinner is fun for the kids. Mostly, I've noticed, folks eat what they are served, so don't stress about it.

Food Swaps

Food swaps are becoming more popular. If my kids were still little, I'd do a dinner swap with my friends. Everybody makes the same meal for a crowd and then swaps it for other meals. So, if there are three families in the swap, each cooks once and gets two swaps—so you get three meals for one night in the kitchen.

Pantry Staples & Purveying

In the words of my health inspector, "A kitchen is a botanic environment." It's the nourishing hub of the home, and it needs to be nurtured with sustainable choices. It's also a place of lifelong learning, connecting us with our families, the seasons, and our communities. Food is life!

I believe we vote with our fork every time we purchase food. Our choices affect our future, and I encourage everyone to support local businesses, farmers, growers, and producers. The less our food travels, the healthier it is to eat and the better it is for our planet. Make friends with your farmers. It's a real treat to prepare food procured directly from the grower, and it does indeed taste better.

As for the nonperishables, let me just say that paperless kitchens are possible. Buy extra cloth towels and keep them handy. Instead of aluminum foil, try using lids, inverted plates, or baking sheets as toppers. I like to find glass CorningWare containers at thrift stores for food storage. And please re-use plastic bags for a second (and a third) go-round.

Finally: compost. Please, compost.

What to Have on Hand

BEANS AND LEGUMES: Please use dried beans instead of canned. Keep an eye out in the fall for dried beans at the farmers' markets. Sprouting your beans is becoming very popular, but it takes some time. It's fine to use canned beans in a pinch.

GRANULATED GARLIC & ONION: These are staples in professional kitchens but rarely seen at supermarkets, although many Walmarts carry them. Fortunately, they're easy to find at penzeys.com, thespicehouse.com or webstaurantstore.com.

LOCAL PRODUCE: Of course! Eat seasonally, locally, and deliberately. It takes seven years to go through the organic certification process. Many farmers are in the process and pesticide free but cannot post the label. Have a chat with them at the markets to find out about their practices.

MEATS: I recommend purchasing local and organic meats directly from a farmer or a reputable butcher who buys from farmers.

OLIVE OIL: I use extra-virgin olive oil for everything. I consider the Mediterranean diet to be my beacon of truth and I don't worry about overheating or the strong, fruity flavor in milder foods. Try grapeseed oil if you prefer a milder oil.

SALT: I mostly use a medium-grain sea salt. Note that if you're using a finer-grain salt, like table salt, you should use a little less, and you might want to use a little more if you prefer a grainier kosher salt.

Vegan Staples

Here are a few of the magic ingredients that can help transform any kitchen into a plant-based wonderland of good eating. Faux meats are handy to have in the freezer, although I don't cook with them much.

COCONUT MILK: Available in cans and a great substitute for heavy cream. If you don't shake the can, the cream that rises to the top is nice and thick.

FLAX EGG SUBSTITUTE: One tablespoon ground flax plus three tablespoons water equals one egg. Combine and let the flax activate before using.

NUTRITIONAL YEAST: Sometimes called "nooch," it's available in bulk bins at natural food stores and also prepackaged. The yeast is typically grown on molasses, but sometimes whey is used, so check if you're feeding a vegan.

VEGAN BUTTER: Earth Balance Buttery Spread is an excellent butter replacement, and its Baking Sticks work well for baking.

PIE CRUST 101

I confessed somewhere in these pages that I buy pie crust for when I cook at home, so I asked my pastry chef Dillard to share his knowledge. Here is his amazing recipe. To make it vegan, simply substitute vegan shortening and vegan butter for the dairy products.

Makes 2 9-inch pie crusts

2 1/2 cups all-purpose flour
1 teaspoon salt
2 tablespoons sugar
1/2 cup or 1 stick (8 tablespoons) shortening, frozen and cut into
   1/2-inch cubes
1 1/2 sticks (12 tablespoons) unsalted butter, cut into cubes and frozen
7 to 8 tablespoons ice water

Few things made in the kitchen are as daunting as pie crust, but the fact is, it's as easy as pie once you get the hang of it. All recipes stress 4 necessary instructions, and I will stress them as well:

1. Freeze the shortening and then cut into cubes before using; as for the butter, it can be frozen after you cut it into cubes.
2. Use ice-cold water.
3. Neither over- nor under-moisten the dough.
4. Do not overwork the dough by kneading it too much.

Many recipes use the shortcut of a food processor. Yes, you will get a good dough, but you will not learn to "feel" when the dough is just right, and this feeling is the great cook's reward. Plus it makes for a flakier and tastier crust. But don't feel bad if you decide to use the processor anyway.

FOOD PROCESSOR METHOD

Put flour, salt, and sugar in processor bowl and pulse a few times. Add cubes of shortening and butter and pulse until a coarse meal forms, about 8 to 10 times. You want the butter and shortening to have little pieces in the meal. Now pulse in the water, one tablespoon at a time, until the dough is just moistened. It should look crumbly.

OLD-FASHIONED METHOD

Whisk together flour, salt, and sugar in a medium mixing bowl. Add butter and shortening cubes to flour. Working quickly and using a pastry cutter, cut in the cubes until the mixture resembles a thick meal. The cubes should now be the size of small peas. Sprinkle the mixture with water, 1 tablespoon at a time, and mix with your hands. This way you'll know when you have the perfect amount of moisture. The dough should feel crumbly.

FINAL STEPS

Next, regardless of the method you've chosen to make the dough, it's time to knead it.

Dust a clean surface or a large bowl (if you don't have good counter space) with flour and dump the crumbly dough on the flour. Using your hands, push the crumbs together, forming a large ball. Flatten the dough ball with the palm of your hand into a large circle, just until the crumbs come together. Fold the dough in half and then in half again and form into 1 large disc. Wrap the disc in plastic wrap and refrigerate for at least 1 hour or for up to 3 days.

Before rolling out the crust, take the disc out of the fridge and let sit for 10 minutes to soften enough for rolling out.

Dust a clean surface with flour, take the disc out of the wrap, and cut in half. (If you only need 1 crust, wrap the remaining disc in plastic wrap and refrigerate or freeze for later.) Flour a rolling pin and roll dough out to a 1/4-inch thickness. Alternatively, you can roll the dough between 2 large pieces of plastic wrap, which prevents sticking and the risk of over-flouring. Gently press dough into a pie pan, trim the edges, and crimp them. The crust is now ready to be filled.

PAR BAKING

If you're going to use a wet filling in your pie or tart, as with the Vegan Pumpkin Pie (page 152), par bake it first. Line it with parchment paper or foil, weight with rice or pie weights, and bake for 15 minutes at 350°. Remove weights and parchment, and bake another 5 minutes. Now it's ready to fill.

A Guide to the Staple Recipes

These recipes can work with many dishes and menus, and most can be made in advance and held at the ready. In my opinion, all mayonnaise should be homemade and no refrigerator should be without some Boozy Blackberry Balsamic Reduction.

Aioli, 115
Balsamic Vinaigrette, 73
Béchamel, page 37
Boozy Blackberry Balsamic Reduction, 133
Breadcrumbs, 37
Cashew Cream Sauce, 143
Creamy Gravy, 77
Croutons, 139
Mayonnaise, 27
Nu Cheeze, 139
Pie Crust, 186
Roasted Garlic, 51
Roasted Sweet Potatoes, 132
Sesame Dressing, 82

Cookware Wisdom

You don't need fancy new cookware; I find some of my favorites at thrift stores. You should have:

Pans: A 10-inch sauté pan, a 12-inch cast-iron skillet, a small and large saucepan, a 10-quart stockpot, two 9-inch pie pans, a 9-inch loaf pan, an enameled, cast-iron Dutch oven (five or six quarts), and a few rimmed baking sheets will handle almost everything but muffins. Look for heavy-bottomed pans; heavy-gauge stainless is ideal for all but the cast iron.

Gear: I love my mini-chop, my blender, and my salad spinner. A large food processor is nice but not necessary. If you've got a heavy-duty mixer, you'll be happy.

Hand tools: Get lots of bowls in different sizes (again, try the thrift stores). I can't live without my spring-loaded metal tongs and good wooden spoons. Have a couple of long, super-thin metal spatulas, a zester, a hand juicer, and a hand-held mandoline. As for knives, start with a serrated knife and a 9-inch chef's knife or a cleaver (I like my cleaver). You can add more knives as you wish later.

A GUIDE TO THE ADVICE

As my family and friends know, I'm not one to hold back on sharing tips and advice. Here's a thumbnail guide to what's scattered throughout the book.

A Balanced Dinner Party Table, 157
Cooking on Vacation, 106
Cooking with Wine, 59
Dinner Party Advice, 13
Don't Burn Your Soup, 63
Feeding the Family, 45
Food Swaps, 184
Grinding Whole Spices, 50
Happy Hour, 16
How Much Booze? 19
How to Deglaze a Pan, 50
How to Roast a Sweet Potato, 132
My Friend Ketchup, 77
A Little Soup Tip, 61
Miso, 59
Menu Planning, 184
My Complicated Relationship with Corn, 85
Pantry Staples & Purveying, 184
Plant-Based Parties, 129
Practical Advice for Making Soup, 49
Roasted Garlic, 51
Seven Tasty Flavor Profiles, 124
Stock, 50
Tips for Blending Soup, 55
Throwing a Big Party, 66
Vegan Staples, 185
What to Have on Hand, 185
A Word About Appetizers, 89
A Word on Seafood, 71

WHAT'S VEGAN

Other than the obvious meat-based dishes, most everything in the book is vegetarian. Here's a list of what's vegan, including dishes that are easily adapted with a single substitution or omission. I'm not including the beverages here, but note that they're all vegan.

Arugula, Winter Squash & Meyer Lemon, 177
Asian Miso Slaw, 40
Baked Polenta Marinara with Pesto & Tofu Crumbles, 144
Balsamic Vinaigrette, 73
Best Ever Lentil Soup, 57
Boozy Blackberry Balsamic Reduction, 133
Cape Verde Vegetable Soup, 56
Cashew Cream Lasagna with Spinach & Mushrooms, 142
Cauliflower Chive Latkes, 179
Cilantro Crema, 133
Cinnamon Fruit Crumble, 87
Coconut Almond Whoopie Pies, 155
Creamy Gravy, 77
Creamy Mushroom Gravy, 131
Curried Cauliflower Salad, 74
Endive, Avocado & Potato Salad, 137
Farro al Fresco, 84
Fennel Slaw, 136
Grammy's Sautéed Apples, 33
Green Beans with Chile Pecans and Sesame Dressing, 81
Handmade Croutons, 139
Honey Roasted Carrots, 79
Indra's Jaffna Potatoes, 102
Italian Cabbage Salad, 41
Mango Salsa, 35

Massaged Kale & Quinoa, 135
Melissa's Peanut Butter Blondies, 105
Miso Mushroom Barley Soup, 58
Nu Cheeze, 139
Onion Bhaji, 149
Paella (vegan variation), 118
Pasta alla Checca, 169
Pickled Cabbage, 39
Pickled Cranberries, 178
Potatoes Anna, 100
Pumpkin Pie, 152
Quick Polenta, 145
Quinoa Fritters, 130
Roasted Salt & Pepper Vegetables, 148
Roasted Vegetable Ratatouille, 28
Savory Cashew Cream Sauce, 143
Sesame Dressing, 82
Slow-roasted Baked Beans, 25
Spinach for a Crowd, 175
Sunshine Ginger Soup, 64
Sweet Potato Fritters, 132
Sweet Potato Lasagna, 140
Tofu Crumbles, 146
Tomato Basil Soup with Coconut Milk, 54
Traditional Spanish Gazpacho, 113
Vegan Caesar, 138
Vegan Pesto, 146
White Beans & Greens Soup, 52
Wonderful Kale Waldorf, 170
Zuppa Pasta Fagiole, 62

What's Gluten-Free

For those who are avoiding gluten, here's a guide to dishes that are either always gluten-free or can be easily adapted. If you're cooking for someone who's gluten-free but don't know much about it, the basic principle is: no wheat, barley, rye, or soy sauce. But it doesn't mean grain-free: corn, rice, quinoa, and farro are all fine.

Amazing Corn Sensation, 85
Arroz con Pollo y Paella, 118
Arugula, Winter Squash & Meyer Lemon, 177
Baked Polenta Marinara with Vegan Pesto, 144 (omit Tofu Crumbles)
Balsamic Vinaigrette, 73
Basque Red Pepper Chicken, 116
Best Ever Lentil Soup, 57
Blackberry Vodka, 163
Boozy Blackberry Balsamic Reduction, 133
Cape Verde Vegetable Soup, 56
Chef Ma's Old Fashioned, 17
Chicken Cacciatore, 166
Chicken Sausage, 31
Chile Pecans, 83
Chilmark Cocktail, 18
Cilantro Crema, 133
Cold Asparagus with Lemony Mayonnaise, 26
Cole Slaw, 39
Creamy Mushroom Gravy, 131
Curried Cauliflower Salad, 74
Endive, Avocado, & Potato Salad, 137
Exotic Salad, 72
Farro al Fresco, 84
Feijoada, 172
Fennel Slaw, 136
Ginger Concentrate, 21
Grammy's Sautéed Apples, 33
Homemade Ginger Ale, 147
Homemade Mayonnaise, 27
Honey Roasted Carrots, 79

Indra's Jaffna Potatoes, 102
Italian Cabbage Salad, 41
Mango Salsa, 35
Masala Chai, 162
Massaged Kale & Quinoa, 135
Moroccan Lamb Tagine, 92
My Favorite Waldorf Salad, 32
Nu Cheeze, 139
Onion Bhaji, 149
Peach Bellini, 17
Perfect Roast Chicken, 94
Pickled Cabbage, 39
Pickled Cranberries, 178
Potatoes Anna, 100
Quick Polenta, 145
Roasted Potato Salad, 103
Roasted Salt & Pepper Vegetables, 148
Roasted Vegetable Ratatouille, 28 (omit the breadcrumbs)
Sassy Raspberry Salmon, 71
Sausage, Peas and Potatoes, 30 (omit the flour)
Savory Cashew Cream Sauce, 143
Silver Palate Party Chicken, 78
Slow-roasted Baked Beans, 25
Spinach for a Crowd, 175
Sunshine Ginger Soup, 64
Sweet Barbecue Brisket, 98
Sweet Potato Fritters, 132 (see variation)
Tortilla de Patatas, 120
Vegan Caesar, 138 (omit the croutons)
Vegan Pesto, 146
White Beans & Greens Soup, 52

my people

Quotes By:
Page 27 ~ Julia Child
Page 8 ~ Ben Franklin
Page 24 ~ Thoreau
Page 35 ~ Elsie De Wolfe
Page 64 ~ Rick Ingrasci
Page 81 ~ Julia Child
Page 54: JC = Julia Child

My World
Allison, Lindsay
Hayden.
My Johnny.

The International Team of
Molly's Friendly Testers:
Anusha, Jara, Brie
Emily, Jules, Gopi, Talia
Lexi, Tracey and Molly!

Starhawk, Sy
Erik, Jamie, Roy

Pepe, Molly, Dillard
Santos, Martha
Sheila
Gio.

Rachel

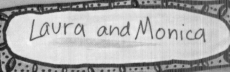

MIRANDA
NATASHA

David

Laura and Monica

Photo Credits:
Page 27 ~ Haejung
Page 29 ~ Kristin
Page 148 ~ molly
Pages 18, 141, 150 ~
mrs. Cook

Best Friends & Role Models
Jen and Gwen, Mimi and Kathleen
Michelle, Colleen, shelley, Betsy
Indra, Melissa, Madonna, Oprah
Luisa, Sue, Lisa, Jo, Debra
Megan, Camille, Delia
Jeanine, Mary Beth, Patti
Stacy, Pauline, Ellen
Martha

Prospect Park Books
Colleen, Jen and Patty

The Becks

Excellent Testers: Ellie, Cathy
Denise, Ana, Ruth, Rikki, Jen
Natalie. Lisa, Emily

THE
AMAZING TIME
BANK TESTERS:
Valerie, Haejung, JL, Mayra
Kindred, Quyhn, Kristin, Sunita, Leann
Howie, Lenora, Julie Ann, Gladys, Paul

PAGE 4 ~ IRISH PROVERB

AMY

My Fitness Team
Keith, Cody, Tracy
MARCO

INDEX

Advice, a guide to, 189
Aioli, 115
Albondigas Soup, 60
Allison's Cookies, 180
Almond milk, 154
Almonds, 74, 84, 154, 164
Amazing Corn Sensation, The, 85
Apéritif, 18
Aperol, 18
Appetizers, easy, 89
Apples, 32, 33, 40, 84, 170
Apples, Sautéed, 33
Apricots, 72, 74, 78, 84, 89
Arroz con Pollo y Paella, 118
Arugula, 84, 177
Arugula, Winter Squash & Meyer
    Lemon, 177
Asian Miso Slaw, 40
Asparagus with Lemony Mayonnaise, 26
Aunt Anna's Corn Fritters, 34
Avocado, 137
Baked Polenta Marinara with Pesto &
    Tofu Crumbles, 144
Ball jars, 87
Balsamic Vinaigrette, 73
Bar advice, 16, 17, 19
Barley, 58, 78
Basque Red Pepper Chicken, 116
Bean dishes
    Feijoada, 172
    Moroccan Lamb Tagine, 92
    Slow-roasted Baked Beans, 25
    White Beans & Greens Soup, 52
    Zuppa Pasta Fagiole, 62
Beans, baked, 24-25
Beans, black, 172
Beans, garbanzo, 74, 92

Beans, green, 61, 81, 118, 148
Beans, pantry advice, 185
Beans, refried, 62
Beans, white, 25, 52, 62
Béchamel, 37
Beef dishes
    Burgundy Beef Stew, 22-23
    Sweet Barbecued Brisket, 98
Bell peppers, 28, 35, 39, 41, 56, 113,
    116, 119, 140
Bellini, 17
Best Ever Lentil Soup, 57
Bhaji, Onion, 149
Bitters, 17, 19
Black tea leaves, 162
Blackberries, 133, 163
Blackberry Vodka, 163
Blending Soup, 55
Blood orange, 122
Bloody Mary, 18
Boozy Blackerry Balsamic Reduction, 133
Bourbon, 17
Breadcrumbs, Homemade, 37
Brisket, Sweet Barbecued, 98
Brussels Sprouts, 148
Burgundy wine, 22-23
Burgundy Beef Stew, 22-23
Buttercream filling, 155
Cabbage, 38, 39, 40, 41, 56
Caesar salad, vegan, 138
Cake batter, 182
Cake, Funny, 182
Cape Verde Vegetable Soup, 56
Cardamom, 50, 102, 162
Carrots, 64, 79
Cashew Cream Lasagna with Spinach &
    Mushrooms, 142

Cashew Cream Sauce, 143
Cashews, 74, 142, 143
Cauliflower, 74, 179
Cauliflower Chive Latkes, 179
Chai, 162
Champagne, 17
Cheese, 36, 85, 89
Cheese, Cheddar, 36, 85
Cheese, feta, 84
Cheese, goat, 72, 84, 89
Cheese, mozzarella, 29, 114
Chef Ma's Old Fashioned, 17
Chèvre (goat cheese), 72, 84, 89
Chicken dishes
    Arroz con Pollo y Paella, 118
    Basque Red Pepper Chicken, 116
    Chicken Cacciatore, 166
    Chicken Sausage, 31
    Miriam's Lacquered Chicken, 97
    Perfect Roast Chicken, 94
    Silver Palate Party Chicken, 78
Chicken Cacciatore, 166
Chicken Sausage, 31
Chicken stock, 50
Chickpeas, 74, 92
Children, feeding, 45
Chile garlic sauce, 71
Chile Pecans, 83
Chilmark Cocktail, 18
Chocolate, 104, 180, 182
Chocolate chip cookies, 180
Chocolate Fudge Syrup, 182
Cilantro Crema (vegan), 133
Classic Béchamel, 37
Classic Potato Croquetas, 114
Cocktails
    Blackberry Vodka, 163
    Bloody Marys, 18
    Chef Ma's Old Fashioned, 17
    Chilmark Cocktail, 18
    Martinis, 17
    Peach Bellini, 17

Coconut, 154
Coconut Almond Whoopie Pies, 154
Coconut milk, 40, 43, 54, 131, 154, 185
Cole Slaw, 39
Cookies, 105, 154, 180
Cookware, 188
Corn dishes
    Amazing Corn Sensation, The, 85
    Aunt Anna's Corn Fritters, 34
    Lentil Soup, 57
Corn, My Complicated Relationship
    with, 85
Cornmeal, 145
Cranberries, 32, 84, 170, 177, 178
Cranberries, Pickled, 178
Cream cheese, 122
Cream cheese, vegan, 133, 138, 152
Creamy Gravy (vegan), 77
Creamy Mushroom Gravy, 131
Crema, 133
Croquetas, 114
Croutons, Handmade, 139
Crumble, Cinnamon Fruit, 87
Cucumber, 89, 113
Cumin Scented Turkey Meatloaf, 76
Currants, 74, 84
Curried Cauliflower Salad, 74
Curry, 65, 74, 149
Deglazing a Pan, 50
Desserts
    Allison's Cookies, 180
    Coconut Almond Whoopie Pies, 154
    Cinnamon Fruit Crumble, 87
    Funny Cake, 182
    Melissa's Peanut Butter Blondies, 104
    Pumpkin Pie (vegan), 152
    Rustic Fruit Tart, 122
    Sticky Toffee Pudding, 42
    Whipped Cream, Vegan, 152
Dinner party advice, 13
Divine Summer Elixir, 21
Double Dutch, 10

Dressings
    Balsamic Vinaigrette, 73
    Caesar, vegan, 138
    Sesame Dressing, 82
Drinks, non-alcoholic
    Chai, Masala, 162
    Divine Summer Elixir, 21
    Ginger Ale, 147
    Ginger Concentrate, 21
    Lemonade, 20
    Watermelon Hearts, 20
Earth Balance, 155, 185
Eggplant, 28
Endive, 137
Endive, Avocado & Potato Salad, 137
Exotic Salad, 72
Farro al Fresco, 84
Feijoada, 172
Fennel, 94, 136
Fennel Slaw, 136
Fish, 71
Flavor profiles, 124
Food swaps, 184
Fritters
    Corn Fritters, 34
    Quinoa Fritters, 130
    Sweet Potato Fritters, 132
Fruit dishes
    Blackberry Vodka, 163
    Boozy Blackberry Balsamic
      Reduction, 133
    Cinnamon Fruit Crumble, 87
    Grammy's Sauteed Apples, 33
    Mango Salsa, 35
    Peach Bellini, 17
    Pickled Cranberries, 178
    Rustic Fruit Tart, 122
    Sassy Raspberry Salmon, 71
    Watermelon Hearts, 20
Fruit Crumble, Cinnamon, 87
Funny Cake, 182

Garbanzo bean flour, 149
Garden School Foundation, 10
Garlic, granulated, 185
Garlic, roasted, 51
Gazpacho, 113
Ginger Ale, Homemade 147
Ginger Concentrate, 21
Gluten-free dishes, 191
Goat cheese, 72, 84, 89
Grammy's Sautéed Apples, 33
Granulated garlic & onion, 185
Gravy, Creamy, 77
Gravy, Creamy Mushroom, 131
Green beans, 61, 81, 118, 148
Green Beans with Chile Pecans &
    Sesame Dressing, 81
Ham, 52
Happy hour, 16
Homemade Ginger Ale, 147
Homemade Lemonade, 20
Homemade Mayonnaise, 27
Honey, 79
Honey Roasted Carrots, 79
Indra's Jaffna Potatoes, 102
Italian Cabbage Salad, 41
Joy of Cooking, 48
Kale, 52, 135, 170
Ketchup, 77
Kids, feeding, 45
Kitchn (thekitchn.com), 50
Lamb dishes
    Minted Lamb Meatballs, 164
    Moroccan Lamb Tagine, 82
Lasagnas
    Cashew Cream Lasagna with Spinach
      & Mushrooms, 142
    Sweet Potato Lasagna, 140
Latkes, 179
Lemonade, 20
Lentils, 57
Loch Duarte Sustainable Salmon, 71

Macaroni & Cheese, 36
Make It & Take It, 150
Mango Salsa, 35
Marinara, 28, 140, 144, 166
Marsala, 58, 59, 131
Martini, 17
Masa, 85
Masala Chai, 162
Massaged Kale & Quinoa, 135
Mayonnaise, Homemade, 27
Mastering the Art of French Cooking, 50
Mayonnaise, Lemony, 26
Meat, sourcing, 185
Meatballs, lamb, 64
Meatloaf, Turkey, 76
Melissa's Peanut Butter Blondies with
    Coconut Chocolate Ganache, 104
Menu planning, 129, 157, 184
Meyer lemon, 177
Mimic Cream, 152
Minted Lamb Meatballs, 164
Mirepoix, 49
Miriam's Lacquered Chicken, 97
Miso, 58
Miso Barley Mushroom Soup, 58
Moroccan Lamb Tagine, 92
Mozzarella, 29, 114
Mushrooms, 58, 131, 140, 142
My Favorite Waldorf Salad, 32
Nu Cheeze, 139
Nutritional yeast, 139, 185
Old Fashioned, 17
Olive oil, 185
Olives, 78, 89, 114
Onion Bhaji, 149
Onion, granulated, 185
Orange, blood, 122
Paella, 118
Pantry staples, 184
Park on Sunset, The, 178
Party advice, 13, 16-19, 66-67, 89, 129,
    157

Pasta dishes
    Cashew Cream Lasagna with Spinach
        & Mushrooms, 142
    Pasta alla Checca, 169
    Sweet Potato Lasagna, 140
    Wednesday Night Macaroni &
        Cheese, 36
    Zuppa Pasta Fagiole, 62
Pasta alla Checca, 169
Peach Bellini, 17
Peanuts, 40, 105
Peas, 30
Pecans, Chile, 83
Perfect Roast Chicken, 94
Pesto, 146
Pickled Cabbage, 39
Pickled Cranberries, 178
Pie crust, 186
Pie parties, 150
Pies
    Funny Cake, 182
    Rustic Fruit Tart, 122
    Vegan Pumpkin Pie, 152
Plant-based Parties, 129
Polenta, 145
Pineapple relish, 172
Polenta, 144
Pork, 172, 174
Potato dishes
    Cape Verde Vegetable Soup, 56
    Classic Potato Croquetas, 114
    Endive, Avocado & Potato Salad, 137
    Indra's Jaffna Potatoes, 102
    Moroccan Lamb Tagine, 92
    Potatoes Anna, 100
    Roasted Potato Salad, 103
    Sausage, Peas & Potatoes, 30
    Sweet Potato Fritters, 132
    Sweet Potato Lasagna, 140
    Tortilla de Patatas, 120
Potato salad, roasted, 103
Potatoes Anna, 100

Pumpkin pie, 152
Quinoa dishes
    Massaged Kale & Quinoa, 135
    Quinoa Fritters, 130
Ratatouille, 28
Rice, 118, 129
Rice milk, 131, 133, 143
Roast Chicken, 94
Roasted Garlic, 51
Roasted Potato Salad, 103
Roasted Salt & Pepper Vegetables, 148
Roasted Vegetable Ratatouille, 28
Romenesco, 148
Root Down LA, 35
Rustic Fruit Tart, 122
Saffron, 92, 118
Salad dishes
    Arugula, Winter Squash & Meyer
      Lemon, 177
    Asian Miso Slaw, 40
    Cole Slaw, 39
    Curried Cauliflower Salad, 74
    Endive, Avocado & Potato Salad, 137
    Exotic Salad, 72
    Farro al Fresco, 84
    Fennel Slaw, 39
    Italian Cabbage Salad, 41
    Massaged Kale & Quinoa. 135
    My Favorite Waldorf Salad, 32
    Pickled Cabbage, 39
    Roasted Potato Salad, 103
    Vegan Caesar, 138
    Wonderful Kale Waldorf, 170
Salmon
    Sassy Raspberry Salmon, 71
    Sustainable Salmon, 71
Salsa, Mango, 35
Salt, 185
Sassy Raspberry Salmon, 71
Sausage, homemade, 31
Sausage, Peas, & Potatoes, 30

Sauces
    Aioli, Super Easy, 115
    Balsamic Vinaigrette, 73
    Boozy Blackberry Balsamic
      Reduction, 133
    Cashew Cream Sauce, 143
    Classic Béchamel, 37
    Creamy Gravy, 77
    Creamy Mushroom Gravy, 131
    Mango Salsa, 35
    Mayonnaise, Homemade, 27
    Pesto (vegan), 146
    Sesame Dressing, 82
    Toffee Sauce, 43
Savory Cashew Cream Sauce, 143
Seafood, 71
Sesame Dressing, 82
Silver Palate Cookbook, The, 78
Silver Palate Party Chicken, 78
Slaws
    Asian Miso Slaw, 40
    Cole Slaw, 39
    Fennel Slaw, 136
Slow Roasted Baked Beans, 25
Slow Roasted Kalua Pork, 174
Sorbet, 17
Soup, burning, 63
Soup dishes
    Albondigas Soup, 61
    Best Ever Lentil Soup, 57
    Cape Verde Vegetable Soup, 56
    Miso Barley Mushroom Soup, 58
    Sunshine Ginger Soup, 64
    Tomato Basil Soup with Coconut
      Milk, 54
    Traditional Spanish Gazpacho, 113
    White Beans & Greens Soup, 52
    Zuppa Pasta Fagiole, 62
Soup, Practical Advice, 49-51
Spain, 111
Spices, grinding, 50

WHO WANTS SECONDS?

Spinach for a Crowd, 175
Squash dishes
    Arugula, Winter Squash & Meyer
      Lemon, 177
    Sunshine Ginger Soup, 64
    Vegan Pumpkin Pie, 152
Staple recipes, 188
St. Germain, 18
Stews, 22, 172
Sticky Toffee Pudding, 42
Stock, 50
Sunshine Ginger Soup, 64
Super Easy Aioli, 115
Sweet Barbecued Brisket, 98
Sweet Potato Fritters, 132
Sweet Potato Lasagna, 140
Sweet potatoes, 92, 132, 140, 172
Sweet potatoes, roasting, 132
Tart, fruit, 122
Tea, 162
Tito's vodka, 19
Toasting Walnuts, 83
Toffee Pudding, 42
Toffee Sauce, 43
Tofu Crumbles, 146
Tomato Basil Soup with Coconut Milk, 54
Tomato dishes
    Pasta alla Checca, 169
    Roasted Vegetable Ratatouille, 28
    Tomato Basil Soup with Coconut
      Milk, 54
    Traditional Spanish Gazpacho, 113
Tortilla de Patatas, 120
Traditional Spanish Gazpacho, 113
TRU vodka, 19
Turkey Meatballs (Albondigas), 60
Turkey Meatloaf, 76
Vegan Caesar, 138
Vegan Cilantro Crema, 33
Vegan cream cheese, 131, 133, 138,
    152

Vegan recipes, a guide to, 190
Vegan Nu Cheeze, 139
Vegan Pesto, 146
Vegan Pumpkin Pie, 152
Vegan staples, 185
Vegan Tofu Crumbles, 146
Vegan whipped cream, 152
Vegetable dishes
    Amazing Corn Sensation, The, 85
    Arugula, Winter Squash & Meyer
      Lemon, 177
    Asparagus with Lemony
      Mayonnaise, 26
    Aunt Anna's Corn Fritters, 34
    Cape Verde Vegetable Soup, 56
    Cauliflower-Chive Latkes, 179
    Curried Cauliflower Salad, 74
    Green Beans with Chile Pecans &
      Sesame Dressing, 81
    Honey Roasted Carrots, 79
    Onion Bhaji, 149
    Roasted Salt & Pepper Vegetables,
      148
    Roasted Vegetable Ratatouille, 28
    Spinach for a Crowd, 175
    White Beans & Greens Soup, 52
Vegetable stock, 50
Vodka, 18, 19, 163
Waldorf salads, 32, 170
Walnuts, 83
Walnuts, toasting, 83
Watermelon, 20
Watermelon Hearts, 20
Wednesday Night Macaroni & Cheese, 36
White Beans & Greens Soup, 52
Whoopie Pies, Coconut Almond, 154
Wine, cooking with, 59
Wonderful Kale Waldorf, 170
Zucchini, 28, 148
Zuppa Pasta Fagiole, 62

About the Author

caterer   mother   *Natur...*   ...vist   *stamper*   ment...

timebanker   doo...   ...ot Down   LA   *tape mak...*

Earth mother   *organizer*   ...en...ded   *shopper* music f...

master food preser...   f...   *permaculturist*   w...

Partner   *artisa...* ...od...   beachbum   *explor...*

boss lady   *party ca...*   ...m...   *Nature lover*   food activ...

...r   mentor timeban...   ...loo...   ... of Root Down   I...

...e maker   Earth mo...   *organizer*   open minded   *shopp...*

...c fan   *master food preserver*   friend   permaculturist   *wi...*

...r *artisan food maker*   beachbum   *explorer* boss lady   *par...*

coordinator   good talk...